PENGUIN

ANY SOU

George Mikes was born in 1912 in Siklos, Hungary. He studied law and received his doctorate at Budapest University. At the same time he became a journalist and was sent to London as a correspondent to cover the Munich crisis. He came for a fortnight and has stayed ever since. During the war he was engaged in broadcasting to Hungary and at the time of the Revolution he went back to cover that event for B.B.C. television.

Mr Mikes now works as a critic, broadcaster and writer. His books include: *The Hungarian Revolution*, *Über Alles*, *Little Cabbages*, *Shakespeare and Myself*, *Italy for Beginners*, *How to Unite Nations* and *The Land of the Rising Yen*. *How to be an Alien*, *How to be Inimitable*, *How to Scrape Skies* and *How to Tango* he wrote in collaboration with Nicolas Bentley, and he has also published a novel, *Mortal Passion*. Many of these have been published in Penguins.

Mr Mikes is married with two children and enjoys getting away from the countryside.

GEORGE MIKES

ANY SOUVENIRS?

Central Europe Revisited

PENGUIN BOOKS

Penguin Books Ltd, Harmondsworth, Middlesex, England
Penguin Books Australia Ltd, Ringwood, Victoria, Australia

First published by André Deutsch 1971
Published in Penguin Books 1973

Made and printed in Great Britain by
Hunt Barnard Printing Ltd, Aylesbury
Set in 10/11pt Baskerville

To my sister, Hédy, and my brother, Tibor
– two other Central Europeans

CONTENTS

CZECHOSLOVAKIA

HUNGARY

WHERE ARE YOU, CENTRAL EUROPE?

WHEN the Iron Curtain descended, Central Europe ceased to exist. People go on talking of Western Europe and Eastern Europe but the Centre has gone. Vienna is of the West; its erstwhile twin-city, Budapest – with similar people, similar traditions, and in the old days, similar coffee-houses – is of the East. Central Europe seems to be unlamented, even forgotten, except by me. I still hold that Central Europe has contributed something to European civilization – yes, but what? I believe that there is such a thing as a Danubian culture – but does anyone else? I insist that Central Europe has a face of its own – but what does it look like now? So off I went, trying to rediscover its contours.

Whatever 'Central Europe' may mean to me the phrase has always had a somewhat comic ring to Anglo-Saxon ears. The Central European is an excitable man with a mop of hair, wearing a long overcoat; a man who talks far too much with a very strange accent. This description, however, is more characteristic of the Anglo-Saxons than of Central Europeans. The Anglo-Saxons are citizens of the world, which means that they have a pretty parochial outlook. They regard themselves as the standard of excellence and people who differ from them – Germans, Scandinavians, Hottentots, Japanese, Italians and Eskimoes – are supposed to be funny. They often are, of course, but Anglo-Saxons regard them as funny *because* they are different from them. The Anglo-Saxons also consider one another – the English, the Americans, and vice versa – the funniest of all; and both the English and the Americans smile patronizingly at the Australians. So studying Anglo-Saxon attitudes towards Central Europe will not help us much.

*

If I were a learned German scholar I should be at great pains to define what Central Europe is. I could speak of latitudes and longitudes. I could say: 'Countries in such and such a geographical position, not bordering on the sea.' But this definition would exclude Yugoslavia and I want to count Yugoslavia in. It would, on the other hand, include Switzerland and I want Switzerland out, simply because I have already written a book on the Swiss. Northern Italy, around Milan, is also nearer to *Mittel-Europa* than to Sicily, yet it is not real Central Europe, it is Central Europe with a strong Latin accent. Or I could take the Habsburg Monarchy for a starting point. But I do not want to be the author of yet another nostalgic book about the Habsburg Monarchy, particularly as I do not feel nostalgic about it. German culture – the cultural space between France and Russia – may be another interpretation, but this is too vast for my purpose. Besides, West Germany has shifted too far to the west; and it can be fairly stated that the culture of these vast regions is not purely German. The Danube could be another hopeful basis for a definition. Indeed, my starting point is Bavaria, where the Danube rises, and I have included Austria, Czechoslovakia, Hungary and Yugoslavia, all Danubian lands. But I feel that Romania and Bulgaria have little to do with Central Europe: they are in the Balkans.* If you retort that Yugoslavia is also in the Balkans, I bow my head. It is. But Yugoslavia is the scene of an interesting and exciting experiment while Bulgaria is deadly dull even among Russian satellites. You may, of course, accept all this as personal idiosyncrasy, and I don't deny that it lacks the solid scientific justification characteristic of a great German scholar.

So I might as well leave the Germans and turn to the

*Transylvania is not; the old Rumanian kingdom is.

Austrians: among them to Karl Lueger, Mayor of Vienna at the turn of the century. He was an old-fashioned, pre-war anti-Semite, not an attractive character. He had – like all Central European anti-Semites of the old school – many Jewish friends and when he was reproached for these connections he gave the famous reply: 'It's up to me to decide who's a Jew and who isn't.' Lueger was one of the heroes of Adolf Hitler and he is no hero of mine; but there is one single leaf I wish to take out of his book. It's up to me to decide what is Central Europe and what isn't – at least in my own book.

*

I was born in Central Europe two years before the First World War and left the place for good one year before the Second. I have lived longer in the West than I lived in the Centre. Now, returning for my first long visit, I found that Central Europe has changed in two essentials: it has lost one thing of importance and gained something new.

It has lost its coffee-houses. The coffee-house in Central Europe – an inheritance from Turkish times – was not just a coffee-house, not just a place where people came to drink innumerable cups of poisonously strong black coffee at all times of the day and night: it was a way of life. People went to these coffee-houses two or three times a day, spent hours on end there, read the newspapers, discussed business and politics, were greeted as *habitués* by reverent head-waiters and received their confidential mail there. The coffee-house was, in fact, more than a way of life, it was a culture. Literary movements of historic importance were born in some of them; notorious crimes planned in others; political debates went on endlessly, political parties were formed and governments were sent packing. The Hungarian Revolution of 1848 began in a coffee-house. The politics of the coffee-house are essentially different from the politics of clubs, of political salons, of the market place or of charcoal burners' huts. Just as the frequenter of the coffee-house belongs to a different species from, say, those New Yorkers who eat their hamburgers standing up and, having swallowed the last gulp of their weak, creamy coffee, rush on to chase more dollars.

In the days when coffee-houses flourished, the chase produced no cash. Today the coffee-houses, as I knew them, are closed. One or two survive but they are merely relics of a bygone age. They may do a roaring business but as a way of life the Central European coffee-house is dead. It is dead on both sides of the Iron Curtain: as dead in Vienna as in Budapest, as dead in Prague, as in Zagreb, so its death is of sociological but not ideological significance.

It was not the demise of the coffee-house that changed Central Europe: it was changes in Central Europe that killed the coffee-house. The coffee-house was associated with lots of leisure time and with huge, spacious buildings. The Age of the Rat Race divides leisure and work sharply. There are times when you must work and other times when you must – well, not enjoy yourself, but 'have fun'. You cannot lounge about in coffee houses between two and four p.m. every day. And the meaning of the word *space* has changed, too. Today it conjures up interplanetary travel, not large, smoke-filled cafés with marble tables where people read the daily papers held in large wooden frames. Certain civilized institutions of the recent past – the coffee-house is one of them – are as dead as feudalism or the Inquisition. Deader, when I come to think of it.

*

What Central Europe gained – if that be the word for it – is the Russians. People keep complaining about 'Russian Communism' but the trouble with Russian Communists is not that they are Communists but that they are Russians. Had Karl Marx been right and had Communism gained power in Germany first and then been tempered by French and British influences, we could today have a reasonably civilized Social-Democratic Europe, with Harold Wilson as its Brezhnev. The Russians are likeable, good-natured, emotional people with great Slav souls, and no people are less suitable for scientific regimentation than they. The trouble with present-day Communism is not that it took the land and the factories from private owners and closed the Stock Exchanges, but that it must remain, by necessity, an oppressive tyranny. Russia had already suffered tyranny under the Romanovs and the horrible years of Stalin's madness only made things worse. Tyranny needs tools of oppression to keep itself in power: either the army, or the political police or both. The régime of the political police backed up by the army is a more important characteristic of Russian rule than the abolition of private landlords or dividends.

Not that Central Europe was a land of ideal, blissful democracy before the Communists came. Bavaria and Austria were Nazi lands and Austria was a fascist country even before Hitler arrived on the scene. Hungary was semi-fascist and feudal, Yugoslavia a royal dictatorship, hopelessly poor and backward. Czechoslovakia was the most decent of the lot, the most industrialized, the most democratic – with some blemishes and flaws here and there. She was bullied, betrayed and carved up. Yet even in Central Europe the arrival of the Russians put the clock back many decades. Today Russian-occupied Central Europe does not just lag behind the West any more: it tries to keep ahead of the Soviet Union. Central Europe used to be the place where the West ended; today it is the place where the East begins.

On top of it all, Communism is a failure as an economic system. It saddens my heart that it should be so but it would be difficult to deny it. People behind the Iron Curtain are badly fed, badly clad, badly housed and all their propaganda organs can do is to envy and denounce the 'materialist' West in the name of an ideology which ceased to be an ideology long ago and has become a means of furthering Russian policy. The internal régimes of the Russian-run countries are tyrannical; from the foreign-political angle the Soviet Union is an old-fashioned imperialist power – where you cannot get enough meat and the razor blades leave your beard still firmly in place.

'But we have a genuine respect for the Russians, all the same,' a Hungarian friend told me. 'If you are shut in a cage with a gorilla so that you have to spend your life with him, you are bound to respect him.'

The presence, or the nearness, of the Russian gorilla is the overwhelming experience for all Central European states. The entire character of the state is determined by its relationship to the Russians. Bavaria had only a fleeting acquaintance with them. Austria – Felix Austria! – succeeded in getting rid of them but she has common frontiers with two Iron Curtain countries and thousands of refugees have poured into Austria on two memorable occasions. Yugoslavia broke with the Russians successfully and courageously and this breach was one of the outstanding events of post-war history. Hungary tried to shake them off by force and was taught a bitter lesson. She knows today that she must live with the Russians, there is no way of getting rid of them. She may achieve compromises, small improvements, clandestine flirtations with the West, but only by accepting the basic fact: the country has moved to the east, into the Russian orbit. Czechoslovakia – twelve years after the Hungarian Revolution – tried to be cleverer and more subtle but was taught an equally bitter lesson. She is still licking her wounds.

The Russian Empire covers a vast and varied area. Czechoslovakia is still a much more advanced country than Kazakhstan. The impression you gather depends on the direction you come from. Should you, for example, arrive in Budapest from Vienna, it looks drab and dreary; should you get there from Warsaw or Moscow, it is the land of your dreams. Russians are as eager to come to Budapest as Hungarians are to go to Paris.

*

Central Europe used to be a nostalgic place for me. A visit to a place cures you, as a rule, of nostalgia. It is never good to pursue memories, ideals and your youth. I found a very different Central Europe from the one I remembered. In a sense I failed to find it at all. During my journey I often felt inclined to believe that people's natural instinct had, once again, been right. Central Europe had, in fact, disappeared. Vienna *is* of the West and Budapest *is* of the East. Budapest is one hundred and fifty miles away from Vienna but it is also one thousand eight hundred miles away: the distance between Moscow and Paris. But Central Europe is still my homeland; I am still an unrepentant Central European. I love the people, I love my mother tongue, I love the scenery, I love my friends. I am worried about the disappearing act Central Europe is putting on but I remain a faithful and loving son of my evanescent parent.

[illegible] to match it all. During my journey I often inclined to believe that [illegible] families had [illegible] General [illegible] had, in fact, [illegible] of the Weser and [illegible] one hundred and fifty miles [illegible] Vienna itself is [illegible] thousand eight hundred miles away [illegible] the distance between Moscow and Paris [illegible] Central Europe [illegible] the people [illegible] any other [illegible] the [illegible] Central Europe [illegible] and [illegible] government [illegible]

BAVARIA

THE PRUSSIAN INVASION

BAVARIA is the Yorkshire of Germany. When a foreigner visits Huddersfield or the East Riding he thinks he is in England. No one will actually argue with him on this point but he will, in fact, be in Yorkshire. The people he meets will not protest – not too loudly, anyway – when he describes them as English; but they will refer to themselves as Yorkshiremen. To be a Yorkshireman implies being English; but it is something more, something better, something infinitely superior.

The Bavarians are Germans and they will not actually deny it. But, above all, they are Bavarians, the one large, nationally conscious ethnic unit within Germany, looking down upon other Germans almost as haughtily as other Germans look down upon them. (Perhaps Württembergers are similar, but Swabian nationalism cannot really be compared with Bavarian.)

The Bavarians' great rivals used to be the Prussians. It was the Prussians who overshadowed them; it was the Prussians who forced them into the newly united Germany in 1871, and many Bavarians regard Ludwig the Second (the king who succumbed to Bismarck's pressure) as a traitor; it was the King of Prussia who became Emperor of Germany and who turned the Kings of Bavaria, once principals on the European stage, into attendant lords, 'ones that will do to swell a progress'. Today, the best-selling history-book in Bavaria is called *How Bavaria Came under the Prussian Helmet** and its jacket shows a Prussian

*Bernhard Ucker: *Wie Bayern unter die Pickelhaube kam, 1870–1970*, Sueddeutscher Verlag.

military helmet – not very different, by the way, from some Bavarian military helmets. The book was published in 1970. Foreigners might assume that Prussia has been dead and gone for a quarter of a century and Bavaria is flourishing as one of the constituent lands of Federal Germany. But foreigners, as usual, would be wrong.

The word *Prussian* changed its meaning long ago in these parts of the world. *Prussian* – as used in Bavaria – does not actually exclude Prussians; *Prussians* are Prussians too, but so are *all* Germans who are not Bavarians. Saxons and Rheinlanders, the people of Thuringia and Holstein, all are Prussians. When, after the war, German refugees poured into Bavaria from all over Germany – and indeed from neighbouring countries – the main worry of the Bavarians was not that their country would be overpopulated and starving but that it would become Prussianized.

Provincials in every country of the world hate (and envy) their capital. You will be told that London is not Britain, that New York is not the United States (I know . . . I know . . .), that Rio de Janeiro is not Brazil. The Bavarians will state with even greater emphasis and fervour that Munich is not Bavaria. It has become a completely international town with all those Prussians – i.e. Saxons, Thuringians, Pomeranians, Balts, etc. and Swabians. Swabians are not Bavarians but they are not Prussians either. Only God and the Bavarians know what they are. At the same time, you will be told that Munich is the true capital of Germany, with Berlin ageing and decaying in isolation. In other words, Munich is the true capital of Germany but not of Bavaria.

This anti-Prussian prejudice is slowly dying out, at least as far as using the word goes. You can still find a few elderly Bavarians who sigh: 'Those were the good old days, when you were permitted to shoot at the Prussians!' Quite a few will quote the old saying: 'North of the Danube [formerly Franconia] is abroad; north of the Main [Prussia] is hostile territory.' The Berliners would retort: 'The Bavarians are the outcome of God's abortive attempt to turn Austrians into Prussians.' This mutual prejudice has, by now, become rather a joke; yet its residue remains. 'The Bavarians are boorish peasants,' the Ruhr industrialist will declare, and the Bavarians accept the slur with defiant pride.

Young Bavarians are not preoccupied with such petty nationalist thoughts and – they say – couldn't care less. They love the French, like the English, accept the Americans and even put up with the Prussians. But I suspect that what looks like a new attitude is largely a matter of terminology. Bavarians speak less and less of *Prussians*, but they speak a lot of *North Germans* – meaning the same thing: that detestable race comprising all other Germans. The North Germans are, above all, the Düsseldorf businessmen who come and buy up Bavarian land; they are the latest menace to Bavarian purity. The Düsseldorf director already has a villa in Sicily and another in the Ticino, Switzerland, but now he buys the third a little nearer home, in the beautiful Bavarian mountains where he speaks (more or less) the language. The Bavarians say that they are slowly becoming a North German colony. The Swiss could forbid foreigners to buy further property in their country but the Bavarians cannot keep out these foreigners from Hamburg, Düsseldorf and the Ruhr.

The dissident murmur of the Bavarians is just a murmur at the moment – and I shall return to this subject later on. The newcomer or the short-term visitor will hear little of it. He will be impressed by the busy, bustling life in the Bavarian cities – above all, Munich – and he will be convinced that he is in Germany. This false impression is so general that we ought, perhaps, to take a quick glance at today's Bavaria as if it were really Germany.

SPEND EASTER IN BALI

WE, Germany and I, first met in 1952 when I went over to collect material for a book.* Since then I have visited her frequently and kept a close watch on her. We have both changed a great deal. I have become a little older, she a little younger; I have become a little poorer, she has become much richer. I have become much happier; and so has she. And we resemble each other in yet another respect: we have both travelled a lot. It is, of course, unusual for a country to travel but Germany managed it. When I first saw her, she was well on her way to the United States; she was becoming Americanized at high speed. But she changed her mind about five years ago and returned to Europe. The change is not easily detectable but it is clearly there. Both the heavy German and the American-type furniture has disappeared from the bedrooms and living-rooms and been replaced by Scandinavian pieces. The smoking of American cigarettes is on the decline. American garments, including Bermuda shorts and blue jeans are out and women follow Paris, or wear English-styled mini-skirts. Men have abandoned the typical American trousers and replaced them by those of Italian cut. American neckties are out and English stripes as well as Scottish tartans are very much in. The heavier type of American shoe has been discarded and light, elegant and dainty Italian shoes have been put on instead. Germany, wearing her new Italian-type shoes, has walked back into Europe. Welcome back.

One only has to walk along the main shopping street of any large town to be able to breathe in the riches of

* *Über Alles*, André Deutsch, 1953. A good book, if you ask me.

Germany. Travel agents abound, intriguing advertisements invite you to join package tours to faraway places: spend Easter in Bali, go shopping in Hong Kong, travel around the world in twenty-four days. The advertisements try to shame you into it: you don't mean to say you haven't seen the Indian Ocean yet? Tut, tut, tut . . . Estate agents offer you properties in the Bahamas, in Morocco and Sicily, villas on the Turkish coast of Asia Minor (and, of course, in Bavaria) or yachts for hire in the Caribbean. Or just take Neckermann's – the great mail-order house's – catalogue: 623 pages in glorious technicolour. You can choose from several thousands of suits and coats – from mini through midi to maxi – for men, women and children. You drop a postcard and they deliver to your home a colour TV set, flying fish, tropical birds (flamingoes, pelicans or cockatoos), medieval musical instruments or skin-diving kits; inflatable swimming pools, speed-boats, yachts, racing cars or an observatory, complete with the finest telescope.

The telescope and the villas are more significant than most people think. The Americans are, on the whole, inward-looking people: they keep watching themselves. The Germans are outward-looking; they watch – perhaps too anxiously, perhaps with too large telescopes – others. After two world wars, the Germans have sincerely and finally given up all idea of conquering Europe. Hardly had they done so, when they succeeded in conquering it without even trying. Half of Europe – at least half of Europe in the sun – belongs to them. Where tanks failed, the cheque-book prevailed; where valueless bombers flopped, revalued marks succeeded. That was a blitzkreig too: it took not much more than a decade to accomplish all this. And they have now *almost* achieved something which even Hitler failed to attain: an *Anschluss* with Bavaria.

What about the old clichés? They die hard. But on the other hand they are never born without good reason. How German are the Germans today? To what extent does the modern German you meet in Munich correspond to the image of one born in the last century? This image is now a century old. It was born, or at least conceived, in Versailles, in 1871, at the moment of German unification. Until then the typical German was pictured as a funny, ineffectual, scholarly type, the subject of princelings, fond of sausages and beer, and preoccupied with Beethoven and Bach instead of with politics and war. Then came the image of the warlike, goose-stepping Prussian, stiff, humourless and brutal, trampling on other people's sensitivities and soil. This image was born, lived a century, culminated in the hideous nightmare of the concentration and extermination camp and is now fading.

The modern German – the latest version – is much less Germanic than his predecessor. Some old habits, of course, die hard, particularly in the older people. A taxi driver could not find the house I wanted although I had given him the proper address. Then he discovered that I meant a well-known newspaper's building. 'Yes, that's what I want,' I agreed. 'Perhaps I should have pointed that out to you. I'm sorry.' He was magnanimous: 'Don't mention it. We all make mistakes. We would not be human if we didn't.' In other words he was quite ready to forgive me *his* mistake: it was entirely my fault that he had failed to find the building after having been given the correct address, but he bore me no malice. This type of thing still exists but is getting rarer.

The famous German heel-clicking is out – it died a natural and unlamented death with the Nazis. Wherever you go, phrases like '*bitte schön*', '*danke schön*', 'please permit me', 'may I', etc. are bandied about. A shade too formal and stiff, almost feudal, you feel. Titles and ranks are still respected: they are firm guides, they establish a proper hierarchy. *Professor* – contrary to the situation in the United States – still means something in Germany. *Doktor-Doktors* abound and *Frau Regierungs Oberinspektors* swarm. President Heinemann has three doctorates and his sycophants use all three.

Manners have improved beyond recognition but they often crack under strain. A Hungarian friend whom I met in Munich told me somewhat ruefully: 'Having lived in London for ten years before coming to Munich, I used my best London manners, trying to get a taxi on a rainy day. People pushed me aside, trampled upon me and on one occasion actually dragged me out of the taxi by force. I lost seven cabs that way. Then I said to myself: "Hell, after all, I don't come from London. I come, really, from Budapest." The next taxi was mine.'

A British librarian working in a German town had this to say: 'I meet many of my clients at the bus stop every morning. They bow, they shake hands, they say how pleased they are to see me. They could not be nicer or more humble. When the bus arrives, they butt me in the belly, push me aside, board the bus and leave me gasping on the pavement.'

Militarism? 'The trouble is,' an American officer told me, 'that the Germans are not militaristic enough.' The German army is, undoubtedly, the most easy-going in the world. Recruits can wear long hair and hippy-type beards; they do not salute their officers except their immediate superiors. Most sergeants dread the charge of being rude to recruits, for recruits – members of a citizen army – may belong to the trades union. As George Vine, an English journalist working in Bonn, remarked in his book, speaking of that famous old baton and the soldier's knapsack: the old German soldier could become a field-marshal; the new one may become the secretary of the Trades Union Congress.

Neither are the Germans patriotic enough: they were too mild and self-effacing *vis-à-vis* de Gaulle and the big phrase, the bombast, the nationalistic thunder has been, for some time, more conspicuous west of the Rhine than east of it. Herr Willy Brandt is today perhaps the most popular statesman in Europe. For more than two decades no German has ventured to utter the suggestion that re-unification was an illusion and East Germany might as well be recognized – or at least tolerated, swallowed as a second (or, with Austria, third) German state. Herr Brandt looked at East Germany with fresh eyes and he became the little boy who discovered that this particular Emperor was not quite so naked; if not particularly well dressed, at least he existed.

And do not feel either that if you want to become a German – particularly if you are a woman – you must become fat. The fat German *Hausfrau* is almost as dead as the heel-clicking Prussian Officer with the Teutonic crew-cut. German girls certainly look more wonderful and enticing than ever before. They always had pleasant enough features but today their figures, too, have improved beyond recognition. 'The *Wirtschaftswunder* – the economic miracle – is nothing; the *Fräuleinwunder* is everything,' I heard often. The *Fräuleinwunder* is the miracle of the slim German girls, conscious of their diet and their figures and competing in elegance with any girls anywhere.

When you decide that the time has come to descend deeper into the German character, you will find that there is a basic contradiction and illogicality in the heart of these most orderly and logical people; the Germans have most certainly become less Germanic but this has happened because they confuse certain things. They believe that duty is a pleasure while pleasure is hard work; they watch their own vices with self-conscious concern and have no idea that these vices are human enough, while it is their virtues which are hard to bear.

Hard work is on the decline. Work is not an important subject of conversation, it lags behind sport, jokes, politics and cars. In 1952 a completely ruined room was let to me one morning and by the next day it had been rebuilt and redecorated, complete with lace-covered cushions and Biedermayer porcelain angels playing their harps on my bedside table. Nothing like this could happen now. Today the German working week is one of the shortest in Europe and the Swabians – the hardest workers of the lot – work even less than the rest. Theirs is a religiously mixed region and they observe *all* holidays. You often see a group of workers: six lazy Italians working hard while two industrious Germans watch them.

Joy and leisure, however, are regarded as a duty. Many beerhalls – with their massive Gothic arches – look like temples and that is exactly what they are. When the *time* comes to make merry, merry they make. Carnival-time and the October festivities are times for merriment. 'Be gay!' the command is shouted, and gay they are. 'Abandon restraint!' they are ordered, and all restraint is abandoned. I saw a German executive arrive in a huge Mercedes at a village on the Tegernsee, all gloom and worry, wearing a dark suit with his chauffeur nearly collapsing under the weight of a monstrous briefcase, which he carried from the car into the house. The boss, too, went into his house and reappeared five minutes later, dressed as a Bavarian hunter in leather shorts and a funny hat with a saucy feather; another five minutes later he was singing happy Bavarian folksongs in the *Bierstube* with the village maidens. He was joyful, frolicsome and gay. He had only a few hours to spend in his country house, so he had no time to waste.

The failings of the Germans are human enough, I have no quarrel with them. I find their virtues harder to bear. I am speaking of their punctuality, efficiency, thoroughness, cleanliness and all the other petit-bourgeois virtues which tend to make one smug and priggish. Efficiency is as much admired in Germany as it is despised in Ireland; punctuality as much approved as it is brushed aside in Italy. (7.30 for dinner in Germany means not later than 7.32; 7.30 for dinner in Italy means any time after 9.15.) To make one's door-handle shine is still regarded as the purpose of life in many circles. Yet I am happy to report that parallel with the genius for organization runs a genius for disorganization. You come across it in the most unexpected places. Cologne–Bonn airport, for example, works like clockwork. But when you arrive on an internal flight and try to find your luggage, you find an inferno instead. There are no signs to show which pile of luggage comes from which city: everything is just dumped down in a huge hall and you are on your own. I saw elderly ladies leap across high counters, fat gentlemen plunge and dive into heaps of suitcases and screaming children disappear under trolleys. Perfect Teutonic chaos reigned and it warmed my heart.

The art of conversation does not exactly flourish in this age, and Germany is no exception as regards this phenomenon. Small talk in Britain, as a rule, centres on the weather which has a wild fascination for the British; in America, more often than not, one hears some unsubtle bragging uttered in order to reflect the speaker's affluence, his influence, his son's success or his own intention to build a larger swimming pool. In Germany the most exciting topics are factual. People are prepared to have long and heated arguments as to whether one has or does not have to change trains at a certain station; they can get very heated over deciding which is the shortest car-route between two localities. They would never look up a time-table or a map – that would spoil the argument. I once heard a feverish argument as to whether a place – where two men had spent a holiday together – was ten or fourteen kilometres away from the sea. When one of them asserted that he had covered that distance, whatever it was, faster than the other, I felt sure that blood would flow.

I have made several references to the difference between the older generation of Germans and the younger one. Many observers have made this distinction and this seems to be one of the clichés now out of date. There are not just two but *three* generations of Germans. For some people the war is still on and will, presumably, never end; many others live in the post-war period. The truth is, however, that even the post-war period is over. The war ended a quarter of a century ago. Even those 'innocent German children' – acquitted of responsibility by the worst Germanophobes – who were going to school under Hitler, are today balding, middle-aged men of forty or over. The real youth of Germany was born after the war and for this generation the Second World War is history, just as the Crimean War or the War of the Spanish Succession is history for us. They are modern young people first and Germans only afterwards.

It would be wrong of course, to assume that this treble division in Germany is clear-cut: older people Type A, the middle-aged Type B and the teenagers and early-twenties Type C. Nothing is quite so simple and clear-cut in human affairs, not even in German affairs – the affairs of a race more given to tidiness than most of us. Reaction to health and sex questions proves this complexity better than anything else.

Health is worshipped like an idol in Germany, and in this young and old concur. To be healthy is a duty: so they go and 'take the cure' at various resorts which are always crowded with perfectly healthy people. The higher one's rank, the fancier the illness one is entitled to suffer from and the more expensive the 'cures' one will be allowed to take at the most exclusive resorts. Healthy middle-aged men in other countries travel around the world as a reward for long service with their company; in Germany they will 'take the cure': it is their duty to have themselves serviced, greased and lubricated, and a few spare-parts renewed, to put them in good shape for another few years of service.

I was told more than once: 'If you want to seduce a German girl, all you have to tell her is that it's healthy.'

Yes, sex and health are closely connected.

The Germans, indeed, have found that this is the age of the sex-revolution and that sex is somehow part of democracy. And they are good democrats, second to none. They accept the Sex Age dutifully and do what they can. In their affluent country sex has become big business. A fifty-year-old German lady, Beate Uhse, has become a millionairess thanks to sex: her shops have a turnover of $6,000,000 a year. She sells 1,800 products, all to do with sex, among them a large selection of sophisticated contraceptives and aphrodisiacs, including chocolates, for willing men and for unwilling ladies; she sells so-called 'quick-lift' panties and battery-controlled stimulators for ageing males as well as love-potions and creams for male timing in sexual activity. There are plenty of books on the market about the 'secret lives' of seemingly respectable people and about group-sex, plenty of erotic encyclopedias, handbooks for homosexuals, and an Uhse Book-Club Choice: *Helga and Bernard Demonstrate 100 Positions of Love*. The shops are of the 'serve-yourself' type. The customers are all males (of all ages), as unconcerned and uninhibited as customers in a supermarket – while the assistants are all female, wrapping up your sophisticated contraceptives as if they were wrapping toothpaste or cheese.

Frau Beate Uhse is a social outcast, excluded from clubs and denounced by church leaders, but she regards herself as a missionary and a social educator. Whatever she is, sex seems to have come to stay. Orgies, if not exactly widespread, are gaining ground and are discreetly advertised in veiled language. I met a respectable businessman who admitted that he participated frequently and I asked him why.

'They are not so expensive,' he replied.

As good a reason as any. Yet he added one more: 'And one sits at one's desk all day. One needs a little exercise.'

There are various explanations of the German sex-revolution; this seems to be one of the many. But much more revealing is the explanation offered by psychologists. I have read an essay which declared that the sex-wave in Germany was an attempt to expunge Germany's dark *Vergangenheit* (which simply means *past*, but when you say *Vergangenheit* it sounds more scientific and more sinister). Someone else put it differently, explaining that young Germany was trying to overcome its *Vergangenheit* in bed. (Note: *young* Germany, which has no *Vergangenheit* and no guilt.) According to an even more complicated version the sex-wave is 'a sort of compensation for militarism, which is no longer permitted in Germany.' Perhaps. It so happened that having read these learned essays I picked up an essay on Danish pornography. A psychologist explained that the Danes' unbounded love for freedom was bound to seek new outlets. So that's it. In the case of the Danes it is the laudable love of freedom; in the case of the Germans it is the guilty *Vergangenheit* and a substitute for militarism.

All this suggests a conclusion to me: the Germans may have changed a lot – but in vain. However much they change, for the rest of the world they remain the same. The rest of us refuse to see what is in front of our noses, we see the outmoded picture; the picture we want to see.

FOREIGN ELEMENT

WHEN Bavarians look about them in their lovely land, they see three main types of foreign element.

Munich is the great cosmopolitan capital, the best place in Germany, full of former *Fluechtlings* (German refugees), Prussians, North-German businessmen and property-hunters, as we have seen. The real foreign visitor – like myself – will observe another problem. He will be aware of another type of foreign invasion: the guest workers, as they are called, the huge number of Yugoslavs and Italians, with a sprinkling of Spaniards, Portuguese and Turks thrown in for good measure. These people work as waiters, kitchen-hands, charge-hands, street-sweepers, dustmen and so on. I feel strongly that this development has a very unhealthy side. Germans (like the Swiss and the Dutch and the English, for that matter) tend to believe that they, *as a race*, are superior beings, a cut above performing certain lowly jobs which must be left to lesser breeds. I shall speak of the culinary significance of this invasion a little later; now I only want to point out that these foreign workers cause much less resentment in Bavaria than do fellow-Germans. These guest workers do have their problems, of course, and not everybody is pleasant to them all the time; but on the whole they are needed and consequently accepted. Many Bavarians will tell you: 'They will leave. The North Germans stay on.' It is easy to love strangers. To love thy neighbour, that's the real problem.

*

Schwabing is the artists' and students' quarter of Munich,

with a little bit of Soho – with its many international restaurants – thrown in. Tucked away there are many elegant or not so elegant studios; and this is the place where businessmen from Düsseldorf and Essen set up their girl-friends in smart little flats, to have them available for their weekly visits.

Bavarian nationalists dislike Schwabing and are proud of it at one and the same time. The place has a great deal of charm and is quieter and less violent than similar quarters in New York, Tokyo or even London. Young people walk around barefoot (at least in the summer) and queue up for pizza and shashlik. Young men wear long hair, young girls wear short hair. They – men and women – wear chains, turbans and, occasionally some domestic animal, such as a cat on their shoulders, or an odd bird or two on their heads. They are not violent, not even self-assertive, rude or pushing. On one corner I saw a girl student selling early editions of next day's paper. She was very elegantly dressed but had no shoes on. She was also lovely – the most attractive newsvendor I had ever seen. No one bought a paper but several young men tried to pick her up. She smiled sweetly at non-buyers and would-be picker-uppers alike and went on offering her newspapers for sale with undiminished trust in the human race as if selling the *Süddeutscher Zeitung* in the streets of Schwabing at twenty past midnight were the most delightful pastime any human being could dream of.

I passed a *Bierstube*, a beer-hall, which advertised a hundred and eleven varieties of beer. Finnish, Turkish and Vietnamese beer were specially recommended. A small group came staggering out of the place, giving the impression of having tasted all hundred and eleven varieties. Or was it just a pint of Turkish bitter that did the trick? I stepped inside for a few minutes and discovered that most of the customers were drinking Löwenbräu, the commonest local beer, available in every café or railway buffet.

On I walked. A young student left his group of about forty others, walked up to me and asked if I could spare forty pfennigs for his tram-fare. I said I could spare a mark. He took it and walked off. He was neither arrogant nor grateful; he was neither touched by my generosity nor acted as if he had been entitled to my money. He needed a few pfennigs and I had them – so I helped him. I am sure he would have helped me in a similar situation. Perhaps he will, one day. He either paid his tram-fare with my mark or bought another pint of Finnish beer. He was welcome to it, whatever he did. A natural and human encounter between people belonging to different cities, nations, generations but – difficult though it is to believe sometimes – to the same species.

*

There is a current joke about German feelings towards the Jews which I have heard several times. Two cars collide in the streets of Munich. One driver gets out and asks the other most courteously: 'Excuse me, sir, but do you happen to be a Jewish gentleman?'

'Jewish?' replies the other astonished. 'No, I'm not Jewish.'

The other's eyes flash: 'Then what the bloody hell do you mean by driving like a bloody idiot?'

Yes, the guilt-feeling survives in some people, not only in Germans, but also in Jews. A prominent Jew, a leader of the community, told me: 'We all feel guilty. All Jews living in Germany know that they should not live here. But we are attracted . . . by what? The chances of good living; the language which is our mother-tongue. And also by a love of Germany. Germany, after all, does not consist exclusively of the Nazi past. Or is this rationalization? We should not be here but we are.'

A great deal has been written on the subject of Jews in post-war Germany and I do not propose to say more than a few words about it here.

There is no noticeable (and most certainly no official) anti-Semitism in Germany but there is a new phenomenon, *anti-philosemitism*, which is very different. Immediately after the war, the young generation was perplexed and worried by their fathers' crimes and felt guilty towards the Jews; they wanted to make amends. These were the people who went to Israel and worked in *kibbutzim*, the communal settlements. But the Third Generation – born after the war – no longer feels guilty, and why should it? It feels that it can judge the Israelis as one judges any other people: on their merit. Besides, Axel Springer is the leader of the pro-Zionists and a reaction against him was bound to produce a reaction against his politics. Germans cannot become anti-Zionists, so they became anti-philosemites: in other words, they do not turn against the Jews but *turn against the German philosemites*. There still remains, however, a strong pro-Israeli feeling in Germany at all levels.

Some of it is genuine. Indeed, I think a Bavarian nationalist – a man who most certainly opposed Hitler's atrocities but will always remain an old-fashioned anti-Semite – was right when he remarked that today Germany is Israel's only true friend in the world. I am sure he did not forget the Americans but he probably thought that many Americans were Jews; others needed the Jewish vote; and others again must oppose the Soviet Union in the Middle East. But today's Germany is a true – even if much less powerful – friend. There are, however, a large number of Germans who are pro-Israeli for the wrong reasons. Many Germans cannot help admiring Israeli militarism; they take vicarious pride in it. It is the achievement of '*unser Juden*', 'our Jews', today. The raid on Beirut airport, the removal of an early Egyptian radar station, the occupation of an Egyptian island in the Suez Canal, the general martial attitude of Israel and even the kidnapping of Eichmann deeply impressed them. Some of them may not like the Jews; but they do love success.

THE FREE STATE OF BAVARIA

WALKING about in Austria – in the Tirol or Vorarlberg – you may reach the German border. A signpost informs you: 'FREISTAAT BAYERN' – Free State of Bavaria.

This will puzzle you. Surely, you have reached the border of the Federal German Republic? Bavaria is not a State; and certainly not a Free State. It may be a 'state' as Utah and Nebraska are states in the accepted, indeed official, but loosely applied sense of the word. Bavaria is a *Land*, a constituent province of Federal Germany, with its own parliament and government – presided over by a prime minister – but not an independent sovereign State with its own international borders.

Are these sign-boards relics of a bygone age? Signs no one bothers to remove? Or pointers to the future?

Bavaria is not really the Yorkshire of Germany but her Scotland: a country with its own profile, people, history and frontiers but without sovereignty. Separatist movements are not only insignificant but they are also rather unsure of themselves. There is no storm; there is no reverberating clamour; but there are rumblings and grumblings. Of all the nationalist movements of the world the Bavarian is the mildest and most indecisive. But it exists. There is no outcry for the recognition of the Bavarian language because there is no Bavarian language – although there is a distinct and easily recognizable Bavarian dialect. No West German politician has ever been kidnapped by Bavarian patriots; no Lufthansa plane heading for the Rhineland Palatinate has ever been hijacked to Munich; and not one single bomb has ever been exploded in the cause of Free Bavaria. Even the French-speaking Swiss separatists of Berne – who want to secede and form their own canton, to be called Jura, within the Swiss Federation – managed to explode a bomb or two; deeds of which even some German-speaking Bernese are inordinately proud. The Bavarians have done nothing of the sort. When the new Federal German Constitution was voted upon in the early fifties, Bavarians rejected it at first, and the Bavarian Party openly campaigned for the establishment of an autonomous Bavaria. But second thoughts prevailed, Bavaria accepted the Constitution, became part of Federal Germany and the *Bayernpartei* faded into insignificance. But talks and discussions among Bavarian intellectuals continue, articles and books keep appearing, restating the case for an autonomous or independent Bavaria. The idea of a Free State is far from dead. Munich – a metropolis – is busy making money and does not even hear these whispers; but the old Bavarian families of the capital and even more the people in the countryside keep asking questions and are growing increasingly annoyed by what they regard as a foreign invasion: the invasion by other Germans.

Bavarian independence may be an unrealistic dream but it is not based on chauvinism. It does have economic undertones and some people feel that Bonn does not represent Bavarian interests properly. But the essence of this nationalism is not aggressive, it is purely cultural. Bavaria is a nation in search of its identity which is being slowly eroded. They do not want to conquer anyone, but refuse to be conquered themselves, swallowed up and blotted out. So many foreigners (North Germans) come to the country, that its Bavarian character is being eradicated. This character, they say, is particularly colourful with cultural and historical roots of its own; it may not be important to humanity but it is important to *them* and if the French are entitled to be French and the Ghanaians Ghanaian, why should they not be allowed to remain Bavarian?

But what is Bavaria and who is a Bavarian?

It was the second Proclamation of the Allied Military Government, issued on 19 September 1945, which defined the frontiers of present-day Bavaria – then, in effect, the American Zone. New Bavaria, with slight adjustments, corresponded to pre-1933 Bavaria. (Hitler, determined to centralize his Reich, practically abolished the rights of the individual States in one of his early decrees.) With an area of around 26,000 square miles Bavaria is the largest of the German *Länder* but her population of over ten million is only a poor second behind North-Rhine-Westphalia. The country is crossed by two large rivers (the Main and the Danube), has numerous beautiful lakes, is covered in wonderful forests and her highest mountain reaches about 6,000 feet.

What constitutes a Bavarian is a more difficult question to answer. In what do Bavarians differ from other Germans?

The Bavarians claim that they are less militaristic and more tolerant than other Germans. Those who remember that Hitler's first successes were achieved in Bavaria and recall the Führer's special addiction to the *Hofbräu* and to Berchtesgaden, may frown upon this claim. But the Bavarians insist that *leben und leben lassen* – live and let live – is their guiding principle. To be sure, I have heard one extremely convincing example of this Bavarian tolerance. There was a student demonstration against the Vietnam war. Some observers noticed that a number of the demonstrators were slightly older than the rest, and closer observation yielded the surprising result that these gentlemen, marching with the crowd and shouting 'Ho, ho, Ho Chi-Minh!' were regular members of the Munich police force, dressed in mufti for the occasion. When the Chief of Police was asked if he permitted his men to demonstrate for Ho Chi-Minh in their free time, he answered: 'No. I *order* them to go and demonstrate when they are on duty. This way I can control the demonstration with two dozen men. If they were not to march I would need five hundred men with tear-gas.'

Bavarians dislike militarism, they say, and the Hegelian idea of the State, the adoration of 'duty', has never taken root in their more light-hearted land. They even claim that their Baroque is gayer and less pompous than that of Austria. They are Catholics while the North Germans are Protestants and important religious links draw them strongly towards the Austrians and the German-speaking Swiss. Their Catholicism contains a great deal of superstition and is full of magical and mystical elements, reverence for the dead, respect for fertility. Every society adapts its religion to its own needs and temperament. Christianity in other countries contains other elements of pagan superstitions. Or take Buddhism: in Thailand it is a gentle and attractive creed, in Tibet it is strict, uncompromising and forbidding. Bavaria is essentially an unsophisticated mountain-peasant society, with an almost incredible mistrust of towns and technicians. They are no intellectuals and are proud of it. Why they should be proud beats me, but they *are*. Other Germans do not really like them and they don't care – or so they say. Some regard them as *gemütlich* (happy-go-lucky, jokey, easy-going): people who dress up in leather shorts, show their red knees, have beefy, round faces, play guitar-like instruments, sing folk-songs and are the entertainers of Germany. They accept the image with pleasure or defiance: yes, Bavaria is the only *land* of Germany where folk-songs are still widely sung by many choirs and special folkloristic societies on radio and television. They also emphasize that while about 30,000 North Germans come to live in Bavaria every year, Bavarians do not emigrate. They love their country and stick to it. There are of course Bavarian restaurants – where a lot of noisy Bavarian music is played – in Hamburg and other parts of Germany, but a few restaurateurs and waiters do not create an 'emigration'; they are no more important than the export of gipsy musicians from Hungary or Andalusian dancers from Spain. And Bavaria is the holiday resort, the playground of Germany; it is very beautiful and all it lacks is the sea.

There are, of course, dents in the old image. Bavarians

are beer-drinkers while a lot of other Germans are wine-drinkers. But the difference between beer-drinking Germans and wine-drinking Germans is simply this: the beer-drinkers drink a tremendous amount of beer and nothing else; the wine-drinkers drink a tremendous amount of beer too, but a lot of wine on top of it. Bavaria is the land of sausages. Now, I am a great admirer of the sausage and a great connoisseur; I think one of the saddest signs of decadence in our age is the general decline of the sausage. It was *not* the Bavarians who invented the sausage, but these greatest of all peoples, the Romans; and the most famous German sausage is called a Frankfurter, not a Münchener. The white sausage – Bavaria's pride – is to my mind an abomination, but this is a matter of taste. The fact remains that Bavarian food is the best in the country. Not so good as the food in Austria but better than elsewhere in Germany. Yet, good Bavarian food, too – to the great annoyance and sorrow of Bavarian patriots – is being pushed into the background. Yugoslav workers have successfully, and in great numbers, invaded Munich and one Yugoslav restaurant is being opened after another. The whole of Germany is full of 'Balkan Grills' – and shishkebab is slowly becoming Germany's national dish, beating sauerkraut hands down. Munich is the worst sufferer. Werner Rukwid, a Munich columnist, complains in a sorrowful and nostalgic article that it is extremely difficult today to get liver-cheese or a good white sausage in Munich but there is no difficulty in getting *cevapcici*, *raznici*, *djuvec*, *sama* and other Serbian delicacies. Indeed, you cannot get away from them. In Munich – Herr Rukwid goes on – you can make culinary excursions to Opatija, Split and other places in the Balkans. Even in pure Bavarian restaurants the waitress is not 'Zenzi' any more but 'Jovanka', and 'Herr Ober' – the headwaiter, once upon a time as much the popular image of the nation as the top-hatted bank-clerk used to be of England – speaks broken German and returns to Istria for his holidays. To the writer's sorrow even Afghan dishes have reared their ugly heads on Munich menus and he tells us with a deep sigh that sometimes when he feels like a plate of sauerkraut he has to order a 'Khyber-Pass' instead.

There are other dents in the image almost as serious. The Ruhr used to be Germany's industrial area and Bavaria the agricultural land. But with the decline of coal, the Ruhr has lost its monopoly and with the growing importance of hydro-electric power, Bavaria is becoming more and more industrialized.

Tourism, too, is an industry and here Bavaria is an easy winner. The thinking and caring layer of the population sees the Bavarian Way of Life collapsing and being eroded. There *is* an Austrian culture they feel, but the Bavarian is not half so safe. They absolutely insist . . . on what? They are not quite sure. I discussed this subject with one of the leading exponents of Bavarian nationalism. Bavaria wanted to be 'free' – he said. We were talking German and I asked him, in what sense was Bavaria not free and what was her justification for being freer? He gave me some reasons and then went on: 'And because her people are occupying a *Kultur-Raum* [a cultural space].'

'This has nothing to do with *Lebensraum*?'

'Absolutely nothing whatsoever.'

'Even so,' said I, 'this seems to be a pretty unconvincing argument. *All* nations, nationalities and tribes occupy, after all, a certain space.'

He thought that over, then replied: 'In English you are right. English is a frightfully logical language. But in German *I* am right. And this battle will be fought out in German.'

'LONG LIVE FRANCO-BAVARIAN FRIENDSHIP!'

THERE were two decisive, formative events in Bavarian history which everyone will point out to you, discuss and interpret, according to his own viewpoint: the first is Bavaria's alliance with Napoleon, the second, Bavaria's joining Bismarck's new German Reich.

The first traces of human beings in Bavaria go back to the age of the dinosaur – but we do not know much of these early Bavarians. The Romans came to Bavaria, then disappeared. The beginnings of Bavarian history proper start, according to Hubensteiner,* in the sixth century. Bavarians, speaking of past glories, often point out that the Tirol was – at diverse periods – under their rule. Some go as far as to say with a lot of pride but with little justification: 'But for Bavaria there would be no Tirol.' Or even: 'But for Bavaria there would be no Austria.' The Tirol was first occupied by the Bavarians in the seventh century. This is not the place to go into details about Arnulf, Bishop Wolfgang, Otto von Freiburg, Walter von der Vogelweide and the many wars – religious and otherwise – fought with changing luck. The first Wittelsbach became Prince of Bavaria in 1180 and Kurfürst Max Josef I became the first King of Bavaria in 1799. The stories of the Ludwigs, the Maximilians, the Prince Regent and the foundation of the humorous paper *Simplicissimus* in 1896 (often mentioned among great historical events) make interesting, often exciting and just

*Benno Hubensteiner, *Bayerische Geschichte*, Pflaum Verlag.

as often romantic reading, but they fall outside the scope of this book.

During the Napoleonic wars, Bavaria – feeling threatened both by Prussia and by Austria – had strong French sympathies but had to stick to Austria and share in her early defeats. In August 1801, however, Bavaria concluded a separate treaty with France and the French promised compensation and reparations to Bavaria, at the expense of Austria. Two years later (in 1803) Bavaria received Würzburg, Bamberg, Augsburg and Freising and some territories of Passau. Bavaria fought on Napoleon's side at Austerlitz in 1805 and gained some further territories, including (once again) the Austrian provinces of Vorarlberg and Tirol.

These years brought important internal changes, too. Indeed, they laid the foundation of the Bavarian claim to liberalism and tolerance. French pressure brought about equality before the law, universal taxation, abolition of serfdom and certain constitutional safeguards. In 1809 Bavaria fought, once again, on the side of the French against Austria, but in 1813 – just before the Battle of Leipzig – she made a timely switch, signed the Treaty of Ried, turned against Napoleon and got reasonably well out of the whole affair. She had to give up some territories, but was allowed to keep others and even gained some new ones.

Those were the days. For a few years Bavaria was a more important power than either Prussia or Austria; she was a French satellite, to be sure – but at least not a Prussian or an Austrian one, which seemed a great improvement to many Bavarian patriots. Bavaria gained military glory, yet progressed by leaps and bounds towards western civilization. Napoleon died in exile but – in a sense – never really left the European scene and survived in many traditions, institutions, thoughts, ideas, passions as well as in many French and Bavarian hearts. Bavaria is one of the eastern *lands* of Germany, with a natural interest in, and understanding for, the Slavs and East European problems; but, at the same time, with strong and warm sympathies for the far-away, western French. These sympathies are remembered and, in a curious way, reciprocated, by the successors of Napoleon. When de Gaulle visited Montreal and shouted: 'Long live Free Quebec!' he created a world-wide scandal, the echoes of which still reverberate even after his death. A few years earlier – in September 1962 – he visited Munich and shouted, with outstretched arms: 'Long live Bavarian–French friendship!' His Bavarian audience reacted loudly and emotionally. They understood. But the world, listening in, either did not understand or – worse still – couldn't care less.

After Napoleon – for six decades – Bavaria remained a kingdom of great splendour and fame, a true rival of Austria. When Greece succeeded in chasing out the Turks and gained independence in 1832, it was Ludwig the First's second son, Otto, who was invited to become king of the new Greece. Otto has always struck me as the most Teutonic of all Teutonic names, with a slightly comic ring to it, and so it struck the newly freed Greeks. *Otto* was more than they could bear, so the new monarch's name was changed to *Otho.** The new king arrived in Greece with a large retinue. The overwhelming majority of those who accompanied him stayed in the country and today, after almost a century and a half, their descendants are as Greek as Prime Minister Papadopoulos himself. Most of them do not speak one single word of German. But, as a rule, they have kept their German names and they are still known as 'the Bavarians'. Otho himself was not a great success. In fact, thirty-one years after his arrival, he was chased away, retired to Bamberg and became Otto once again.

The other traumatic event of Bavarian history is Bismarck's war against Prussia, followed by the declaration of the New German Empire. The Bavarians had good reason to remain neutral in 1870–71. They knew that Bavarian independence was much more threatened in that war than French independence. Besides, their traditional friendship

*Greek scholars – classical and modern – please do not write to me explaining the letter *theta*. I know. The fact remains that Otto has been turned into Otho.

for Napoleon Bonaparte was naturally to be extended to his nephew. But for Ludwig the Second (as for almost all kings – and all presidents, prime ministers and party leaders, for that matter) the chief consideration was not the *Salus Rei Publicae*, the supreme good of the state, but his own power. There was little doubt that the new Emperor of Germany would very much remain King of Prussia. Ludwig had weighty reason for not entering the war and, later, not joining the Empire. But staying out might have meant the loss of his throne; and to remain King of Bavaria with limited powers was incomparably better than being chased away. So, love of Napoleon or no love of Napoleon, a Bavarian army marched against France under the command – to add insult to injury – of the Prussian Crown Prince. (This was not the incident which de Gaulle had in mind when he shouted: 'Long live Bavarian–French friendship!')

Within the new Reich Bavaria was second only to Prussia and gained certain concessions which other States would not have dared even to demand. She retained a separate diplomatic service (a Bavarian Minister was sent even to Berlin), a military administration, a postal, telegraph and a railway system of her own. Yet that scene in Versailles – the proclamation of German unity – was the end of true Bavarian glory; Bavaria went on existing but ceased to count. Ludwig – as I have already mentioned – is regarded as a traitor by many Bavarians. They say he sold out to Prussia and became her subject to save his throne. This may indeed have been his intention; but, whatever his thoughts and fears, he only bowed realistically to the inevitable. Ludwig's 'choice' was more apparent than real. History knocked on Bavaria's door and she had to accept Prussian overlordship. Yet modern Bavarian historians maintain that 'the victory of all German forces in 1871 also made the catastrophic defeats of 1918 and 1945 indivisible.'* (Indivisible, of course, means: it involved Bavaria in the private affairs of Prussia.) Ludwig went on ruling with

*Bernard Ucker, op. cit.

circumscribed powers for another fifteen years. In 1886 he became insane, Luitpold was appointed Prince Regent on 7 June, and Ludwig the Second committed suicide six days later. He survived all blows to Bavarian prestige so long as he remained king; he did not survive the loss of his throne. Which shows, perhaps, that he was less insane than they thought.

HOW INDEPENDENT?

WHY is it that the world takes seriously the national aspirations of small African or Asian tribes, of every tiny island in the Mediterranean, but smiles benevolently – or laughs aloud – when the national aspirations of the Bavarians are mentioned? Surely, *every* nation is entitled to search for its identity, to be different from others and add some more colour to a uniformly drab world?

Herr Ucker points out that there are quite a number of countries in Europe which are smaller or only slightly larger than Bavaria. Belgium and Holland are less than half Bavaria's size, Switzerland and Denmark a little more than half. Eire is about as large and Austria and Hungary not considerably larger. That is the position in Europe. If we take the whole world, there are one hundred and thirty-nine sovereign States of which ninety-nine (71 per cent) are smaller than Bavaria.

Some patriots tend to dwell on the great Bavarians of the past but they do not fare too well. Richard Strauss, the composer, is the one and only name of truly great stature they can muster. The name of Baader is often mentioned with reverence and awe, but Franz Xavier von Baader was hardly a major figure. A professor of philosophy at Munich in the first half of the nineteenth century, he was a Catholic mystic who talked much of the redeeming love of God. He was a disciple of Boehme – himself a minor luminary and, in turn, a disciple of Paracelsus. Baader is not even mentioned in Bertrand Russell's *History of Western Philosophy*. Neither is Boehme. Then follows a large gap and the next great Bavarian seems to be Gabelsberger, the inventor of shorthand. Now, shorthand was a very useful innovation and full marks to Herr Gabelsberger. But this is the type of invention somebody else would have come up with very soon if Gabelsberger had not thought of it. I hate to boast, but I myself would almost certainly have invented short hand, had I not been forestalled by the great Bavarian. And now there ensues another great gap until we reach Herr Franz Joseph Strauss, leader of the Christian Democratic Union, the greatest living Bavarian. Not a tremendously impressive list.

In all fairness, perhaps I should add that there are many very good Bavarian orchestras, singers and performers on various musical instruments, but I could not find one single famous Bavarian writer. A man called Frauenhofer invented some optical improvements and Karl Steinheil constructed the first electric clock. Bavarians also invented the *Weisswurst*, the white sausage, and the first *Oktoberfest* (the great beer-drinking festivity in *September* when the whole country gets drunk and goes completely mad) was held in 1810.

Two remarks should be added to all this. Firstly, the number of great men produced by a nation has little to do with its true worth; and still less with its right to independence. Why should people constantly justify themselves, boast about their achievements and the contributions they have made to world culture? The right to be mediocre is one of the basic human rights. Bavarians are called mountain-peasants by inhabitants of other *lands*. They accept this description: 'Yes, that's what we are; that's what we intend to remain.' Secondly, Bavaria has an outstanding record for providing a refuge and a spiritual home for real giants who were persecuted in their homelands or who simply preferred to work elsewhere. Röntgen, Dürer and Wagner are only three of the names which come to mind.

How independent does Bavaria want to be? The degree varies, even among Bavarian nationalists. There are some who simply remark nostalgically: 'Munich is the best city in Germany. That's our tragedy.' Meaning, of course, that the pleasantness of Munich attracts too many North Germans and it would be better if they stayed at home. Others speak – or dream – of an Alpine Federation, or of some vague, undefined Alpine community consisting of Bavaria, Austria and the German-speaking parts of Switzerland: all mountain people and all Catholics. Others again are in despair. One of these told me: 'We live in a vacuum. Bavarians, as a nation, have ceased to exist. And to crown it all we are doing too well, making too much money, so we've lost interest in minor problems, such as our country and our survival as a nation.'

Another man prominent in the movement for Bavarian nationalism had this to say: 'The trouble is, that we are no flag-wavers. Two wars, especially the second, have taught us to hate flag-waving, goose-stepping and rhetoric. And no nationalism can be truly successful without both the beating of drums and the beating of chests. We are nationalists who hate the very word *nationalism.*'

The precise up-to-date meaning of *nationalism* preoccupies them. It is a cultural nationalism they are after. They do not want a Bavarian Empire, they do not wish to conquer parts of the Rhineland Palatinate or Baden-Württemberg, but they do want to keep their Bavarian character and ancient culture and in order to do that, they feel they need a larger degree of autonomy than they have at present. Some say that political frontiers ought to disappear completely, all over Europe, while cultural frontiers need to be strengthened. When I asked about the possible dangers of Bavarian nationalism, one of their leading intellectuals, a very learned gentleman, pointed out: 'Bavarian nationalism is harmless. It is *German* nationalism that is dangerous. Greater Germany might lead to a new Reich. The secession of Bavaria would serve European peace.'

There is a minority – a small but important, highly educated and articulate minority – who speak of the possibility of secession. 'What's good for Austria is also good for Bavaria.' – 'If Switzerland can be independent, why not Bavaria?' – 'We have our *Staatsbewusstsein* – our consciousness of being a nation; we have our individual Way of Life; why can't we go on in our own way?' – 'Federation? Yes, perhaps. But that is our minimum demand. It would have to be a true Federation, very different from the present one.' Or: 'Federation? Yes. But it must be an independent Bavaria which decides, of her own free will, whether she wants to federate or not. And why should we federate with Germany? Why not go straight into Europe?'

During these discussions, I recalled how disappointed I was, in 1952, by the German attitude to German unity; unity between East and West Germany. Almost everybody paid lip-service to the idea and no one, except the eighteen million East Germans, wanted it. (Today, even they do not want it.) No one ever spoke up against unity in public: not one single politician, not one single newspaper – until, rather late in the day, Herr Willy Brandt broke the ice. Many of the Bavarian nationalists are openly against the unification of Germany. I have already mentioned the gentleman who pointed out the dangers of German nationalism versus Bavarian nationalism. Another man remarked: 'No German unification. No, thank you. Centralization is the greatest danger. Centralization might lead to a new Reich – a tragedy for Europe, a tragedy for the world, a tragedy for Germany.'

This made sense, politically. So I was surprised when a well-known extremist of the Bavarian nationalist group declared himself strongly in favour of German unity. The most determined amongst them declared emphatically: 'Germany has a right to unite. It is immoral to keep the nation divided. There is not one single valid argument I can think of to keep Germany divided.' He looked at me: 'You seem to be surprised.'

'I am,' I replied. 'Do I understand you to say that you want unification first and then you want a free Bavaria to secede from a *united* Germany?'

For a moment he looked taken aback.

'Damn you. It is not a kind way of putting it. But yes, I guess that's what I want.'

AUSTRIA

THE LAND OF SMILES

MODERN Austria is an unknown country and a lucky country. The libraries of Britain contain dozens of books on her catastrophic collapse in 1918; scores on the Austrian Empire; hundreds on the Habsburgs. But I could not find one – not one – book in English or French on modern Austria since World War Two. People know about skiing in Kitzbühel and about the Salzburg Festival, and the highly cultured may have heard of the White Horse Inn on the Wolfgang Lake but there their knowledge ends. The whole world knows about Dubcek who was Party Leader in Czechoslovakia for a few months; people even know the name of his unhappy successor, Husak; they have learned the name of Kadar, the Hungarian Party Leader and President Tito is, of course, one of the few statesmen of world stature. These are politicians of small countries, bordering on Austria. But what does one know about Austrian politics? I am not criticizing others for I blushingly admit my own ignorance. I, born next door – indeed, born as a subject of Austria-Hungary – knew that Austria had been governed by a coalition for more than a decade and that she now had a socialist government. But I could not recall the name of the Chancellor (an interesting and brilliant man, I subsequently discovered) and when an appointment was made for me with the Foreign Minister I had to admit that I had never heard of him before.

Some of the basic facts: Austria lies at the very heart of Europe; her territory is over 32,000 square miles (a little smaller than Hungary) and she has about seven million inhabitants. She has common frontiers with seven countries:

five Western and two Communist. The Danube flows through the land for over two hundred miles. We all know by now that the Danube is not blue, but whatever its colour, Austria with her mountains, spas and lakes is one of the most beautiful countries of Europe. She resembles Switzerland. Less developed, less cultivated some say; less spoilt, say others. Nearly 200,000 Hungarian refugees poured into Austria after 1956 and tens of thousands of Czechoslovaks after the occupation of their land by the Soviet Union in 1968. Most of the refugees have left, but a considerable number of them have settled there. In spite of this, 99 per cent of the population claim that their mother tongue is German and nearly 90 per cent are Roman Catholics.

Austria has always had the reputation of being a lucky country. *Bella gerant alii, tu felix Austria nube* said the old hexameter, meaning that other countries had to wage bloody wars in order to steal other people's territory while lucky Austria did it through the judicious marriages of her Habsburg princes. Austria's luck held. She is the only country in modern history which the Russians left of their own free will. Khrushchev wanted to prove that Russia was a kind and civilized power, beautifully suited for co-existence. This attitude lasted for but a few minutes in historical terms, but Austria benefits from this passing whim.

An Austrian politician told me the following (Austrians, as we shall see, love to describe their history in jokes, anecdotes, witticisms, and parables): 'You know the famous old joke? A very poor old Jew goes to the rabbi and complains to him that he cannot bear the overcrowding any more. He, his wife, his father, father-in-law, mother-in-law and five children live in one small single room. What should he do? The rabbi thinks hard and tells him: "Let the goat in, too." The poor man can scarcely believe his ears but the rabbi repeats his advice. So he goes home and does as he was told. A week later he returns and complains that life is utterly unbearable and not worth living. "Let the goat out," suggests the rabbi. The fellow rushes home, takes the goat back to its shed and after that enjoys every minute in that wonderful little room which houses only nine human beings.'

'You've got it?' my informant asked. 'Poor Austria had two goats in her little room. First the Nazi goat, then the Russian goat. Now that both have gone we are consciously and gloriously happy to have our little place to ourselves. Positively happy for negative reasons. We are the happiest country in Europe.'

You could, of course, argue a point or two. The Nazi goat was *let in* – like the goat in the story – while the Russian goat came uninvited. Others would argue that the Nazi goat, too, was an intruder. There is no doubt, however, that whatever the manner of their goats' intrusion, the Austrians are extremely happy to be rid of them. Happier than their neighbours, the Czechs and the Hungarians who still have the Russian goat in their drawing-room; but also much happier than their other neighbours, the Swiss who do not know what it is like to have your home turned into a goat-shed.

During my tour of Central Europe I visited Austria twice: once coming from Britain via Germany and later on the way back from Hungary. As a result, I saw two different places: an Eastern country first, a Western Paradise later on. When you are dipped into tepid water, you feel – in normal circumstances – that it is what it is: tepid water. But if you were first immersed in ice-cold water, it would feel hot; if you had previously been pushed into boiling water it would feel ice-cold.

Vienna, when I arrived from the West, gave the impression of being charming, beautiful, well-off, yet a smallish city with a tinge of the Eastern and a strong touch of the Central European. People's manners are obsequious, over-polite, yet with a thick layer of ill-disguised arrogance beneath this exaggerated courtesy. The shops are elegant and well-stocked but the selection is well below that of Munich's. You can get wonderful shoes or pullovers but your size may be out of stock: perhaps they can get it within a fortnight; perhaps not. There are plenty of books in the bookshops but the well-known and important volume you are after may happen to be sold out everywhere, all over the city. They might or might not order it from Munich and it might or might not arrive in two weeks. Or three. I heard a man ask for a book on etymology in a great Viennese bookshop, mentioning the title, author and publisher. The assistant looked it up in the latest catalogue and replied: 'Sorry, there is no such book.' The man took the book out of his briefcase, showed it to the assistant and told him he wanted another copy of it. The assistant grew angry and banged his fist on the catalogue: 'It's no good showing me the book. It just doesn't exist.'

Many people will tell you that Austria is becoming, especially culturally, a part of Germany. Authors publish their works in the land of Big (and Rich) Brother and successful journalists are lured across the border by the attractions of much larger fees and a wider readership. Shoppers swarm over to Germany – some small German border-towns actually depend for their living on Austrian shoppers; the goods may be dearer but the right size is always available over there and what you actually want is already in stock and available.

After a few days in Vienna you will become aware of that famous mixture of people which is one of the most typical and most bewildering characteristics of Central Europe, or true *Mittel-Europa*. Near the village where I was born – across the border, in Hungary – we had eleven neighbouring villages, all of different nationalities: a German (Swabian) village; a Serbian; a Slovak; a Croatian; and others of lesser known tribes such as the Shokats, the Bunevats and so on. (There was, surprisingly, even a Hungarian village among them.) The name of a family I met recently in Vienna exists in five versions (German, French, Dutch, Czech and Hungarian). Members of the family live in all the five countries. In Yugoslavia there is a village where one side of the main street used to be purely German, the other side purely Serbian. You needed no passport to cross the road but each nationality stuck to its own side. After the expulsion of the Germans, Montenegrins were settled there, and one side of the street became theirs. But the newcomers hated the life of the plains and returned to their beloved mountains. Hungarians – from the Voivodina – took their place. Today, one side of the street is still Serbian, the opposite side is Hungarian – strict apartheid is still observed.

The story is told (it is an invention but could be true) that a man born in those regions was asked: 'Where were you born?' 'In Hungary.' – 'Where did you go to school?' – 'In Czechoslovakia.' – 'Where did you go to high school?' – 'In Hungary.' – 'Where do you live now?' – 'In the Soviet Union.' The other is duly impressed: 'You must have travelled a lot.' – 'Not at all. I never left Uzhorod.'

The town of Uzhorod (Ungvar) belonged to Hungary until 1918; then it became part of Czechoslovakia; Hungary got it back after Munich but had to give it up to the Soviet conquerors after World War Two. There is nothing very unusual about such stationary travelling in Central Europe.

It is enough to walk along the corridor of an Austrian ministry and look at the name-plates, or just to study the telephone-book, to see an incredible pot-pourri of German, Hungarian, Czech, Slovak, Polish, Rumanian, Dalmatian, Croatian, Serbian, Italian, Bosnian, Macedonian and Albanian names – some Germanized, some just bastardized, some in their original form. This is the inheritance of the Empire; also the result of recent turmoil.

I returned to Vienna after spending five weeks in Hungary and found myself unmistakably in the West. There was nothing Eastern, or even definitely Central European, in Vienna any more. The shops looked elegant, well-stocked and alluring. The bookshops were truly cosmopolitan. What if a title or two was not available? The main thing was that political censorship did not exist and every publication – from the USA to China, from London to Moscow – *could* be there. Indeed, one often sees penniless Hungarians walking along the Kärtnerstrasse, admiring the shops with envious, incredulous eyes, running from one window to another as if they had arrived in a dream world.

Yet it took me quite a few days to grasp what the *real* difference was. I had arrived in the *Land of Smiles* - not in the operetta but in the true sense of the word. It was only in Vienna that I realized: in Hungary no one had smiled. They had laughed, of course, they had often laughed aloud; and often at very good jokes or truly witty remarks. More often they laughed at silly badinage, at childish teasing, at cheap irony. It was the polite, friendly smile which was completely lacking: the gentle smile, the other fellow's joy at seeing you, the smile of the eyes, not of the lips. Here in Vienna, round-headed, beer-drinking men with fat red faces kept smiling at you. They might be less witty than their neighbours across the border, and less sophisticated; but if they were silly, they were silly enough to be able to enjoy life.

SCHLAMPEREI

SHOULD you discuss the Austrian character with any Central European, two German – nay, Austrian – words will immediately crop up: *Gemütlichkeit* and *Schlamperei*. Both words can be explained and defined but no corresponding single words exist in English. *Gemütlichkeit* is gaiety, geniality, lightheartedness, joviality and *joie de vivre* rolled into one, with a dash of frivolity added. *Gemütlichkeit* is not simply a passing mood, a temporary state of mind, it is a *Weltanshauung*, a way of contemplating the world. It is Western – indeed, Austrian: the opposite of oriental contemplation – a smiling shrug of the shoulder, a couldn't-care-less attitude, a belief that this may not be the best of all possible worlds, but here we are and we might as well make the best of it: even positively enjoy it. It is not fatalism: or rather, it is fatalism carried one important step further: acceptance of your fate with good spirits, with a broad smile. It is a mixture of simple-mindedness and sophisticated simplicity. Life, death, bankruptcy, wars, the fate of dynasties, are tragedies; but they are also jokes played on you by fate. *Gemütlichkeit* is *not* the courage to laugh at adversity: it is the belief or recognition that adversity is just as much fun as fun itself. You may drink *heuriger* wine and sing ribald songs in the company of your cronies, accompanied by *Schrammelmusik*, or else you may go down with flu. But whatever you do, you may as well enjoy it.

Schlamperei is the special Austrian version of inefficiency. It contains elements of carelessness, muddle, negligence and slovenliness but it also contains elements of *Gemütlichkeit*. Yes, things are very bad, in hopeless confusion: but who cares? Why not laugh at them instead of getting angry, developing high blood-pressure and suffering heart-attack? Should you discuss Austrians with Englishmen, instead of with Central Europeans, they will almost inevitably quote the notorious assessment of the strategic situation of an Austrian general during the First World War: 'The situation is hopeless but not serious' – a perfect fusion of *Schlamperei* and *Gemütlichkeit.* It was most probably the Austrian's cheerful inefficiency which brought about the situation; but once it was upon them there was no need to take the threatened loss of the battle, of the war, the collapse and dismemberment of the Empire and the expulsion of the Habsburgs after seven hundred years as if it were something important.

In Vienna I went to visit the Intendant – the administrative director – of the Austrian State-theatres including the Opera. This is a very high position indeed and the gentleman in question, I am told, fills it extremely well. But we did not discuss Austrian theatrical or operatic art at all. He gave me a copy of his own book: the history of Austria in jokes. The title proclaims: *Greatness is Dangerous**: and the commendable idea behind the title is that the great men of history should be laughed at, or their funny remarks should be appreciated, and in this way they should be brought down to a more human level. The sub-title is: *True stories from the history of a difficult nation.* I started reading with great interest and went on with growing irritation: does the author think that all history is a huge joke and nothing else? Does he think that history is simply raw material for a few people's witty remarks about battles, wars, national disasters, dynastic problems? But my mood changed again. I read the book twice, enjoyed it very much and was convinced, in the end, that if the book is not history (which it does not purport to be), it is a useful corrective to history. Some people see life as an unending tragedy; more superficial people regard it as a joke. The wisest know that life is a synthesis: every great tragedy is funny; every joke is tragic.

*Gottfried Heindl: *Und die Grösse ist gefährlich*, Paul Neff.

Herr Heindl remarks in his preface that the anecdotes reflect the humour of a people who are not really gay but simply ready to make fun of everything, especially of themselves. The Austrians keep belittling themselves, he says, but as Bismarck noted: 'They make themselves appear small lest we see how big they are.' Be that as it may, the book is full of stories like this: in 1915 there was a lot of trouble in connection with the Polish region of Galicia, and the Governor of Moravia – who was responsible for the province – complained to Redlich about his problems. 'Don't you know,' asked Redlich, 'what the basis of future peace settlements will be? Whoever loses, gets Galicia.' When a general mood of hopelessness filled the air in those days and people seemed ready to throw in their hands, Prince Ludwig Windischgrätz quoted the old cavalry officers' saying: 'You can play cards without money; you can't play cards without cards.' Even more typically Austrian: when Charles, the last Habsburg, ascended the throne in 1916, after the death of Francis Joseph, in dark and ominous times, some literary gentlemen in Vienna tried to invent a suitable motto for the new Emperor. One of them suggested: 'In my domains the sun never rises.'

So much for the classical notion of *Gemütlichkeit* and *Schlamperei*, and the synthesis of the two. The idea has always been, of course, that *Gemütlichkeit* is pleasant and laudable while *Schlamperei* is an evil to be got rid of. My impression is the reverse: down with *Gemütlichkeit* and long live glorious *Schlamperei*.

In the first place I have always viewed Austrian jollity with a great deal of suspicion. It is partly genuine, of course, but partly it is artificial. Many Austrians know that they are supposed to be *gemütlich* so they play the part. You meet with a large amount of genuine helpfulness. You can scarcely study a street map of Vienna without someone accosting you and offering his help. Perhaps two or three people will volunteer their version of the shortest way to the Opera or the Votiv-Kirche, and will quarrel among themselves as to whose route is the best. We stopped near the

Ballhausplatz (Vienna's equivalent of the Quai d'Orsay, where the Foreign Ministry is situated) to admire some statues. An elderly gentleman dressed like a cross between a Tyrolean hunter and an old-fashioned university professor came up to us and asked: 'Are you foreigners?' We admitted the charge. He – in a somewhat prolonged lecture – explained all about the statues, told us the history of Hercules, bringing in quite a few marginal details of Greek mythology about Amphitryon and Iphicles, and then, turning to another statue, began a dissertation on Admiral Tegetthoff and the role of the Austrian Navy in the Adriatic. He had reached the battle of Lissa when he caught sight of two American girls looking at Hercules on the other side of the road. He left us without saying good-bye or even nodding and trotted over to the girls. 'Are you foreigners?' we heard him ask. We departed in frustration. We shall never know who won the Battle of Lissa.

But perhaps the most helpful and solicitous of all Austrians I met was the shoeshine boy in my Vienna hotel who woke me at 6.30 on my first morning there, demanding the shoes I had forgotten to put out. (In fact, I did not forget, but I have strong objections to letting other people clean my shoes. I hate seeing these humiliating, personal services being performed, but in Vienna, for the rest of my stay, I suspended my principles and put my shoes out.)

A typical Austrian manifestation of common-sense and wry humour was their official order when Arab hi-jackings of Israeli planes became fashionable. The airport authorities decreed that El-Al, the Israeli airline, was to park its planes at outlying points of the airport, away from other aircraft. A sensible arrangement: this made it much easier to detect anyone approaching the planes. The special Austrian touch came when they also decreed that Arab planes were to be parked beside the Israeli ones. The idea was that if the Arabs started shooting they would, as likely as not, hit their own planes. Should they – the Austrians reasoned – destroy their own aircraft, their heroism and the gratitude of their people would be greatly diminished. Perhaps Karl

Kraus, the brilliant Viennese writer and wit, knew what he was talking about when, hearing someone remark that the Austrians had hearts of gold, he mused: 'Yes, I always suspected that their hearts were made of some heavy metal.'

How much better and more heart-warming is *Schlamperei.* It was in the Austrian provinces that I saw the (presumably) unique zebra-crossing which led only half-way across the road. Perhaps when the work was half-finished the men went away for lunch and never returned. And only in Austria could an airport hotel be so misleadingly signposted that it took half an hour to find, and then be shut when you found it.

In the troubled days of 1938, Schuschnigg, the Austrian Chancellor, ordered a plebiscite to decide whether Austria should remain independent or should join the German Reich. It was in response to this that Hitler invaded Austria and no one heard another word about the plebiscite. Except one Tyrolean village. It had not heard of the *Anschluss.* It duly carried on with the plebiscite and sent in the results to the central authorities, by then in Nazi hands. The village had voted unanimously against the *Anschluss.*

After my expulsion from Hungary, I gave a press conference in Vienna and the news item was carried in scores, perhaps hundreds, of newspapers all over the world, all correctly. It was only the Viennese *Die Presse*, whose correspondent was actually present at the press conference, which succeeded in getting more errors than facts in the piece. The writer got the date of my expulsion wrong; he said that the BBC had been expelled with me, when I had emphasized about five times that this was not the case; he said that I was a 1956 refugee although he had been informed both orally and in a handout that I had left Hungary in 1938; that I had written a number of books on Hungary's political developments when I had written none; and – for good measure – that I was also expelled from Hungary in 1964 although I had made it clear that on that occasion I had been well-received and treated like royalty. *Die Presse* is reputed to be Austria's best-informed and most reliable newspaper.

And yet I am on the side of *Die Presse* and of Austrian *Schlamperei*: they warm my heart. The Austrians - and this is one of their most lovable traits - appreciate the small pleasures of life. Surely, lifeless, soulless cold efficiency has nothing to do with small pleasures. Why should we become slaves of the clock, of computers, of the rat race and suchlike silly details when enjoyable chats, good friends, a steaming *Mocca* (the most popular version of Austrian black coffee), a piece of *Sacher-torte* and a good laugh are the things that really matter in life? Who cares in any case whether I left Hungary in 1956 or 1938? And why should that zebra crossing run right across the road? Half-way is enough: some sort of indication is sufficient. People will not think that pedestrians may be freely knocked down on the unpainted half. Austrian students do not protest, do not sit-in, do not build barricades and are not up in arms. Not because they are satisfied with this wretched world but because they cannot be bothered. Protests lead nowhere, except to a refreshing *Mocca* afterwards. So they might as well cut out the demo and have the coffee straight away. *Schlamperei* is civilization; efficiency is decadence.

Schlamperei is also improvization. It is dealing with problems when they emerge; crossing bridges when you come to them; mending holes when they are right under your feet.It is pragmatism, in fact, so it should be an English virtue too.

It is, of course. An Austrian official who had witnessed the scene, told me that during his state visit to Britain, the President of Austria went to have the inevitable lunch with the Lord Mayor. He was received in splendour, with grace and hospitality. When the Lord Mayor proposed the toast, he referred to Austria four times as Australia. At the end he lifted his precious cut-crystal glass and proclaimed in ringing tones: 'Long live Australia!'

'English *Schlamperei*,' I remarked.

The Austrian official shook his head: 'Don't blame the English. They are innocent. It's all our fault. Our *Schlamperei* is infectious.'

I wish it were.

ROUGHLY SPEAKING

I BOARDED a tram in Vienna and asked for a ticket to the Opera. 'But that's only one stop,' I was told by a strongly disapproving conductor. 'Well . . .' I said apologetically, being thoroughly ashamed of my sybaritic ways. Taking a tram for one stop – really. I handed him the money but he refused to take it. He could not accept money for such a short ride. What the rules and regulations had to say about taking money was a consideration which, I feel sure, never even entered his head. It was *morally* wrong to take the tram instead of walking a few steps. I stood corrected. Never again did I dare to take the tram for only a single stop.

You often meet this paternalistic type of kindness. The Austrians are good-hearted, helpful people but they also educate you, tell you off and run your life for you.

I liked Vienna, was impressed by it and said so to my many Viennese friends. All loved Vienna more than I did but all contradicted me. No, it was a small town; provincial; a minor West-German city. Oh no – people were not half so nice as I thought. Austrians were terrible drivers; cars made life unbearable; true, the view from the hills was beautiful and the Vienna woods lovely but it was becoming more and more of a strain to get there. When I conceded any one of these points, they were deeply hurt. It took me some time to realize that they did not really mean to criticize Vienna at all. Their remarks had nothing to do with negative feelings towards Vienna; they expressed rather the positive joy of grumbling – one of the Austrians' basic human pleasures.

This habit differed sharply from the practice I was to meet in Hungary. Often, in truly wretched circumstances, Hungarians praised the flaws and failings in their lives and tried to explain away the hardships; they tried to persuade me that life was better, richer, freer than it really was. Also that they were much better off than they really were. Because they are a proud people, trying to hide their poverty, they all became propagandists of a régime which many of them loathe. Austrian grumbling grew from different roots. For a long time they lived as the master-race of an Empire, they were allowed to enjoy themselves but not to interfere in politics. The *Kamarilla*, the secret police, was ferociously oppressive as soon as people expressed interest in public affairs. There was no free press and many subjects of conversation were taboo in public. So they grumbled. Grumbling became their basic human right; the last vestige of freedom; the reassuring sign that they still remained free citizens.

Behaviour towards others is courteous – indeed annoyingly over-courteous. The manners of waiters, hotel-staff, shop assistants and so on have a slightly feudal flavour, implying a great deal of respect, indeed humility towards you, which appears (and is) completely phony. I cannot blame them. Why should they – or anyone else for that matter – revere me? Just because I enter a shop to buy a hat or choose a certain restaurant in which to eat boiled beef? People – quite rightly – resent the servile attitude they are expected to adopt so they mix a few sly digs with it. Outwardly they remain polite; in essence they make it clear that they do not think much of you. These pin-pricks and contemptuous overtones do not amount to much but they are obviously there and you come up against them a dozen times a day. You cannot put your finger on anything concrete and – even if you were thus inclined – you could not complain to the manager. You ask a question in a shop and you get a perfectly polite reply as far as the actual words are concerned, but the tone implies: what a bloody fool you must be to ask such a stupid question. Or you walk out of a shop without buying anything – or having bought something very cheap – and a chorus of ironical *Auf Wiedersehens* accompanied by mock bows will pursue you to the street.

In spite of all their charm, gaiety, kindness and – often genuine – politeness there is another rather irritating trait to be found in the Austrian character. Not even their best friends could say that they are extremely quick on the uptake. They are a mountain people and an honest people. Mountains – with their limited horizons – slow down one's thoughts and honesty slows them down still more. It is only the poor vagabond living on his wits and always after a quick buck (or lira) whose mind is sharp and quick. He has to think fast just to survive; the well-to-do honest mountain-peasant can afford to ponder and chew over every little detail.

I was often tempted to finish people's sentences for them – they meandered along so slowly and the gist was so obvious. And many Austrians take everything quite literally. I heard a story about a Hungarian refugee, a girl with a job in a small tailoring business in Vienna. About a dozen other women worked there, among them Frau Reiner. This Frau Reiner was poor, fat, middle-aged and very dull even by the standards of that workshop. One day Frau Reiner failed to turn up for work and the manager informed the other women that she had gone to Holland for an indefinite period. This caused a major sensation around which the conversation revolved for several hours. Had anyone been told that Frau Reiner planned to go to Holland? No one had. So she went quite unexpectedly? Just like that? And why to Holland, of all places? After an hour and a half of this type of speculation, the Hungarian girl who could not stand it any longer asked them: 'Did you see in the newspapers that Queen Juliana is ill?'

One or two had read the item.

'Well,' said the Hungarian girl, 'perhaps Frau Reiner was asked to go to Holland to stand in for the Queen for a few days.'

This suggestion was received in silence. At first, the others seemed to be impressed. Quite a career, to be sure. Then one or two of the brighter ones started expressing their doubts: 'Frau Reiner? . . . To Holland? . . . To stand in for the Queen? . . . But why Frau Reiner? . . . No, that is unlikely . . . Yes, it *is* unlikely.'

Another half hour and it dawned on them all *how* unlikely it was that Frau Reiner – a machinist in a small firm making ladies' coats in Vienna – should be asked to act as Regent of the Netherlands. What an idea! A ridiculous suggestion! And ever since then the Hungarian girl has been regarded as very stupid.

I ran across some surprising ways of thinking. I was expecting a certain sum from an English newspaper and I knew that it would be sent to me through the *Kreditanstalt* branch in the same block as my hotel. So I went down to the branch to inquire if my money had arrived.

The clerk was eager to help me but explained that they received scores of transfers every day, so it would help if I could tell him which English bank acted for the newspaper.

'I am afraid I don't know,' I replied.

'You don't know?' the clerk asked me, still keen to help.

'Haven't got the faintest idea.'

He thought this over, then he asked hopefully: 'But roughly speaking?'

'Roughly speaking it's Barclays.'

He went to investigate and returned ten minutes later to report that there was nothing for me from Barclays. Was I sure it was Barclays? No, I wasn't sure at all. Could it be the Westminster? Yes, it could. Or Lloyds? Or the Midland? Or indeed, anything? Yes, anything.

'Then why did you say Barclays?' he asked me.

'I spoke roughly,' I replied.

There was a vague look in his eyes, he was obviously unsure as to whether this was a satisfactory explanation or not.

The Austrians also have a genius for stating the obvious at some length. I went into a hotel near the Wolfgangsee at six o'clock on an August afternoon and asked if they had a room. They had none, the receptionist told me. I said 'thank you,' and was about to leave when a lucid explanation followed: 'There are too many guests in the hotel in August. They have taken all the rooms. That's why we haven't got one free.'

On another occasion I asked a kind gentleman where a certain Ministry was. He pointed to the other side of the road, bang opposite: 'There.' I thanked him. He – probably realizing that I was a foreigner – added most helpfully: 'You must cross the road to get to it.'

POLITICS

TODAY the world knows too little about Austrian politics; there was a time when it felt it knew too much. Critics of Austria have stated that she was responsible for one and a half world wars and the economic world crisis of the thirties as well. A number of Austrian patriots – eager to stress the importance of their country – have agreed. But the criticism, or claim, is exaggerated.

The reign of Francis Joseph (1848–1916) was a series of unmitigated disasters, political and private. In 1849 he had to call on the Tsar's help to defeat the Magyars who, with their untrained peasant army, had beaten the Austrians hollow. This victory, with the ensuing carnage and bitterness, proved to be a Pyrrhic one, but it was on the tenth anniversary of Francis Joseph's accession to the throne that the tragic turning point really came. It was in this year (1858) that his ill-fated son Rudolf was born. Field Marshal Radetzky died in the same year and the Emperor took actual command of all Austrian forces and led them from disaster to disaster. The first in the series occurred almost immediately after his taking command. Francis Joseph was tricked by Cavour into declaring war on Sardinia *and* Louis Napoleon's France. The Austrians suffered a disastrous defeat at Solferino in 1859; they lost 40,000 men in dead and wounded, and forfeited huge slices of their Italian territories (indeed, all of them, with the exception of Venice, which they lost soon afterwards). Francis Joseph decided to reverse Metternich's former pro-Prussian policy and to demonstrate Austria's hegemony in the German world. This ended in the defeat at Sadowa (the Austrians refer to this battle as Königgratz and the Slavs, to add to the confusion, refer to it as Hradec Kralove). The defeat was not only decisive but the war was humiliatingly short, it was all over in a matter of weeks. As a result Austria was forced by Bismarck out of the German league and she lost Venice. 'The year 1866 was more than a military disaster for Austria – it was the beginning of the end. It was the end of the established order that Metternich had tried to build up and it was the culminating consequence of Francis Joseph's series of vacillations, experiments and mistakes. Austria was now out of Germany and out of Italy: an implacably hostile Russia was meddling in the Balkans and Hungary was still smouldering.'*

Austria-Hungary (born in this form, 1867) still looked like a great power. The Emperor had more than fifty million subjects (but only twelve million of these were Austrians); his lands enjoyed – after Solferino – half a century of peace. But one private disaster followed another. His brother Maximilian, Emperor of Mexico, was executed by a firing squad. Maximilian's widow Charlotte went mad; Francis Joseph's son and heir, Rudolf, committed suicide in Mayerling and took with him Baroness Marie Vetsera, aged seventeen, with whom he was not even in love; the Emperor's wife, Elizabeth, was murdered by an anarchist in Geneva.

All this created deep – and deserved – sympathy for the unfortunate man, but he deserved no sympathy for one of the stupidest and most pointless blunders of his long reign. The Congress of Berlin (1878) authorized Austria-Hungary to administer the territories of Bosnia-Herzegovina (now part of Yugoslavia). Thus Bosnia-Herzegovina became to all intents and purposes an Austrian province: the Austrians ruled it as they pleased – or as well as they could – and there was no point whatsoever in annexing it. Yet this is what Francis Joseph did – out of the blue, for no good reason. In 1908 Austria issued a declaration about the

*Richard Rickett: *A Brief Survey of Austrian History*, Georg Prachner, Vienna.

annexation of the province, without even notifying her allies, Germany and Italy, in advance. This foolish move nearly plunged the world into war. Volumes have been written about this crisis, but I, for one, still fail to understand the Emperor's political motives. I understand, however, his human motives. He was getting old and was obsessed by the wish to hand over his lands intact to his successor. He had, however, no chance of doing so: he had lost his Italian possessions. So he probably thought he would compensate his heir by providing him with new territories. Like the honest bureaucrat he was, he meant to account for as much territory in square miles as he had received. He would not be found short. His book-keeper's honesty nearly caused a world war – and this in spite of his other obsession, which was keeping the peace.

When the last personal tragedy befell him, the murder at Sarajevo of his heir, Francis Ferdinand, Francis Joseph had his last chance of making up for what he had missed six years before. It would be unfair to say that Austria caused World War One, but her irresponsible ultimatum (prepared by the warmonger Konrad von Hötzendorf and meekly signed by the senile Emperor) was one of the main contributory factors to its actual outbreak in August 1914.

Twenty-four years later it was the occupation of Austria by Hitler which ought to have opened the democracies' eyes to the Nazis' intentions. But they refused to see; their eyes remained closed.

As if all this were not enough, Austria is often accused of having caused the world recession in the thirties. It is true that it was the collapse of the Austrian *Kreditanstalt* in 1931 which sounded the alarm but it is quite unfair to accuse Austria of causing the world-wide economic disaster. She was the first victim of the recession, not its maker.

The *Anschluss* in 1938 made Austria the focal point of world-wide interest. This is not the place to discuss whether Austria's rape by the Nazis was indeed a rape or a love-affair. A large number of Austrians certainly did welcome the Nazis and Hitler's entry into Austria looked like a triumph. He had some initial success: unemployment disappeared in no time and his popularity grew. But disenchantment soon ensued, even for the Austrian Nazis. The *Anschluss* wiped the name of Austria off the map, she became instead *Ostmark*, Germany's easternmost province, and all the juicy jobs went to Germans. What enthusiasm remained quickly disappeared after Hitler's attack on Russia, when several Austrian divisions were wiped out and the war brought untold suffering in its wake. After the war Austria regained her independence but she was beaten, starving, in ruins and under occupation. Reconstruction started. Austria being Austria one of the first things to be reconstructed was the Viennese Philharmonic Orchestra. In those early days the orchestra often had to do without its great conductors and second-raters, indeed beginners, got their chance. Herr Heindl tells us in one of his anecdotes that in those days someone asked the leader of the orchestra about X, a young, inexperienced conductor: 'What is Herr X going to conduct tonight?'

The reply came: 'I don't know what he is going to conduct; *we* shall play Beethoven's Sixth Symphony.'

After Austria's liberation she went through a nightmarish 'Third Man' period of which the rest of the world was aware. The world also knew that the country was divided into zones but was jointly administered by the US, Great Britain, France and the Soviet Union. We got used to seeing pictures of jeeps carrying four military policemen – one from each of the occupying powers – patrolling the streets of Vienna. Some friends of Austria smiled at these pictures; others nodded; others again sighed. It was a sad commentary that all that remained of Allied co-operation at the height of the Cold War was the guarding of Nazi war criminals in Berlin's Spandau Prison and these jeep patrols in Vienna. Karl Renner – Austria's outstanding pre- and post-war statesman – put the matter graphically when he likened his country to a small rowing boat with four elephants as passengers. Another politician summed it up in other words: Austria has always been the home of good wine, good beer and good spirits. France represented the wine-belt, Britain the beer-belt, the Soviet Union vodka and other hard spirits. 'All we have to do now is to fit in the Coca-Cola belt.'

It was in 1955 that the world looked once again on Austria. I have spoken earlier of Austria's good luck due to Khrushchev's thaw, which secured her liberation. In all fairness, one has to add that Austrian statesmanship also played its part. But without good luck this statesmanship could have achieved nothing. In September 1955 the last foreign soldier left Austrian territory and Austria became an independent, neutral, Western country, small and poor but, I am sure, much happier than it used to be at certain periods of her huge, once-glorious empire. Today Austria is just as small as she was in 1955; but she is not poor any more. Not rich but quite well off and the schilling is one of Europe's most stable currencies. More stable than the rouble; steadier than the pound.

Austria's post-war political life is remarkable for the existence of a coalition government in peace time. In the early post-war days, the Russians – who occupied only one zone of Austria – could not turn the country into a People's Democracy but their influence was strong enough to prevent the most odious development in their eyes: the emergence of a proper, critical opposition. This was the origin of the coalition. After the departure of the Russians there was no political reason for continuing the coalition, but there were non-political reasons: Austrian laziness, and their happy-go-lucky nature. The coalition persisted through sheer inertia. No one wanted to change a situation that had worked. It had worked badly; but it had worked.

Forming a coalition government is a remedy often suggested in emergencies of varying seriousness as a panacea. Ideologies are disappearing in any case, everywhere, and managerial politics are taking over in the US as well as in Russia, in Britain, and in France. Why not form a coalition, using the best brains of a nation and to hell with the stupid and outdated game of party politics?

In theory this is fine; but Austria tested this theory for a decade and a half after the Russians left – for a quarter of a century altogether – and her experiences were discouraging. This is what one Austrian politician told me – a Socialist and an academic.

'During the occupation coalition was not only inevitable but also important for Austria. The country was governed by the famous four elephants and only a united Austria could carry some weight *vis-à-vis* the occupying powers. The Right would have met with Russian, the Left with Western hostility. But by 1960 – five years after the State Treaty – coalition had deteriorated into a bad marriage: the habit was much stronger than love. Of course, nothing is purely white or purely black and coalition even in those days had certain advantages. But they were far outweighed by the drawbacks. Everything was settled *in camera*; arguments and quarrels were conducted behind closed doors and the public was not properly informed about the real issues. All decisions *seemed* unanimous but represented merely unconcern, or, even worse, the result of hard bargaining (if you agree to this, I agree to that). People heard only the results, the decisions – never the arguments, never the pros and cons. In such an atmosphere sham problems occupy the centre of interest and the real, grave issues remain the concern of a few professionals. Coalition had other adverse effects: it was hardly ever the right man who got the job but the man who belonged to the right party. If the job had to go to a Socialist it went to one, even if he was the most incompetent of all the candidates. (Or name any party you like – this remains true.) People learned that in order to get jobs they had to belong to the right party and this was bad for the job, for the people, and also for the parties: they became full of people who were absolutely uninterested in the parties' aims and ideals, even in politics in general. They had joined because this was the way to get on in life.'

It was in 1970 that Austria reverted to proper – proper? – party-politics and the Socialists came to power. But old customs die hard. Not much enthusiasm could be whipped up for politics and Austria's political life has sunk into respectable dullness. Perhaps this is a blessing; but the symbol of Austrian political life is not the sword, not the hammer and sickle, not the national flag but the national yawn. Fewer people read newspapers than in any other western country and there are many large families without a single newspaper-reading member. There is not much trouble with left extremists. The Communists cannot make any real impact – Austria has had a taste of Communism and that was enough. Neo-Nazis do not cause much trouble either. As a politician told me: 'Our new Nazis, unlike those in Germany, are the old Nazis. And they are getting very old or are dying out. The whole problem dies with them.'

Political indifference – or ignorance – goes far. Some people declare that even the departure of the Russians made no difference. This is maintained not by Communist propagandists but simply by people with short memories. I heard this peculiar remark so often that I mentioned it in conversation to a member of the Austrian Government who replied with the inevitable anecdote: 'It makes no difference? I don't know ... You have heard about the Jew who appeared in the Synagogue without a hat? The rabbi was outraged. He shouted at him: "In the Synagogue without a hat ... ? It's horrible. It's like ... like ... what shall I say? It's like sleeping with a prostitute instead of with your own wife."

'The man said nothing. Next day, however, he came back and said to the rabbi: "Now I have tried both. You can't really compare the two."'

HOW TO LOSE AN EMPIRE AND STAY HAPPY

THIS is the greatest lesson Britain has to learn from Austria; this is the question that makes Austria specially important for us.

Between the wars Austria suffered a great deal from the after-effects of Empire.

After World War One the country had been drawn and quartered (quartered in the literal sense of the word). One-third of its people lived in the capital; Vienna was Socialist, the country itself semi-fascist, with (later) Nazi elements sprinkled everywhere. Austria faced insoluble political and economic problems and irresistible pressures. All that was left to her was the Imperial Hangover and in this she indulged her injured pride.

The remnants – the memories – of this still survive. Austria still remembers when she was, or looked like, a great power, one of the dominant voices in Europe, in a world where nothing outside Europe really mattered. Many Austrians will still remark wrily that Austria is a country which looks forward with confidence to a glorious past.

The theatre in Vienna is good; but few experiments are going on. Grillparzer, Shakespeare and Raimund are still the favourite playwrights. Music is better still but even more old-fashioned. A curious love for the operetta survives: the romance between the count's youngest son and the beautiful goose-girl, or stories of merry widows and *Csardas* – princesses, with melodious love-songs and with the grand entrance of the *prima donna*. But, curiously, there are no new operettas; it is the old operettas which remain moderately popular. This is the whole point: Austria looks back at the glories of the past although she is ready to accept the realities of the present. With some reluctance, of course, for which she should not be blamed. There are no revolutionary parties, no revolutionary movements, no student revolts, no storming of the heavens. They do not fight for a grand and noble future; it takes enough self-discipline on their part to have given up the fight for a grand and noble past.

Austria is well-to-do, not tormented by strikes and political or balance-of-payment crises. She exports a great deal, mostly in the industrial line but also some agricultural products, and her tourist industry – which, thanks to the wonderful skiing resorts, flourishes all the year around – is decisively important. The country is noticeably less affluent than Germany; and perhaps even rather less affluent than it seems: a great deal of the old, genteel, bourgeois tradition of hiding your poverty survives. That well-known figure in turn-of-the-century short stories and comedies, the poor relation who lives in sham splendour, is not extinct.

As soon as Austria regained her true independence in 1955, she decided to follow a policy of neutrality. This was at the express desire of the Soviet Union but it suited Austria as well. Her main hope and interest was to avoid interference or undue influence from either of the two super-powers.

The shining example to every neutral power is Switzerland. She is the most experienced neutral while Austria is only a beginner. Yet in one important respect Austria refused to follow the Swiss example: she joined the United Nations. Here again she willingly followed the good advice of the Russians. 'It is impossible for one country slavishly to follow the example of another,' the Foreign Minister told me. 'Following even the Swiss example in absolutely every detail would have meant giving up our independence straight away.'

Austria felt that for two long periods – during the Nazi

occupation and during the Allied occupation – she had simply been wiped off the map; she did not exist; she was a non-country. To get back properly into the fold, to remind the world of her existence, it was necessary to join the United Nations. Some people have a strange vision in Austria, just as in Bavaria; they envisage a kind of Unity of the Alpine peoples. There is a long stretch of land in the centre of Europe, from the Danube to the Jura, from Eastern Austria to Western Switzerland, destined to remain neutral come what may. The influence of the countries situated in this area must be felt. If we add to the neutral group the growing, increasingly vociferous, and well-organized (aligning) group of the non-aligned (see the chapter on Yugoslavia) then the possibility cannot be ruled out that one day we shall all come under the tyranny of neutral and non-aligned nations.

Austria's foreign political problems are not gigantic. She had certain difficulties with her two Iron Curtain neighbours; with Hungary after the Revolution of 1956 when 200,000 refugees poured into Austria, and with Czechoslovakia, where there is still the unsolved problem of compensation for confiscated Austrian (as distinct from German) assets. Austria follows the policy of peaceful co-existence with these two countries and, on the whole, succeeds. Relations are better with Hungary than with Czechoslovakia. The Hungarians maintain a much more civilized façade nowadays, and coach-loads of tourists – Austrians and foreigners who leave for Hungary for one or two-day excursions – are important for the Hungarians, so they behave with exemplary courtesy towards Austria. With the Czechs they have the above-mentioned dispute and its visible sign is the fact that Austria keeps a Legation, not an Embassy, in Prague. But the occupation of Czechoslovakia by the Russians and the oppressive neo-Stalinist régime of that country put the clock back by decades, the Austrians feel.

'We do not even look in their direction,' a member of the Austrian Government told me. 'They are on our doorstep, of course; but, in a sense Prague is as far away as Johannesburg.'

At first Austria treated West Germany with suspicion but this suspicion has faded and the two countries are good friends. 'Does anyone think about a new *Anschluss*?' I asked the Foreign Minister. 'Perhaps one per cent of the people in both countries: immediately after the war more people thought seriously about it: we felt lonely in the world; we felt lost; our Europe had disappeared and we had neither friends nor relations. Many people thought that we were doomed to eternal poverty and isolation. That we just couldn't succeed. But we *have* succeeded and we *have* learnt to stand on our own two feet. We need no *Anschluss*.'

Austria has her problems with Italy, too. The South Tirol or Alto Adige (according to whether you call this region by its German or Italian name) was given to Italy after World War One. This act was a major injustice. Lloyd George said so; Winston Churchill said so; Adolf Hitler, the great patriot, did not say so; he sold out the Austrians to Mussolini. The Italians never treated their Austrian minority too well and there is a certain amount of tension – Tirolean bombs even explode occasionally in Italy. But both countries are anxious to remain friends, so negotiations about some autonomy for the German-speaking minority goes on. The Austrians try to hurry them up; the Italians drag their feet.

You can live with such problems. Austria does not maintain any forces East of Suez; has no problems about whether to support the Arabs or not; and is not worried by the fate of the Austrian Commonwealth. There is no Austrian Commonwealth – even less than there is a British Commonwealth and that is saying a lot. Power without responsibility may be the prerogative of the harlot; but seeking responsibility without power is the prerogative of the fool.

Austria is a small European country, accepting her geographical position, dividing her schillings into a hundred groschen, measuring length in metres and weights in kilograms, accepting the fact that Francis Joseph is dead – indeed that he was dead during the last twenty years of his reign – and enjoying her own dullness. We usually speak of dullness derisively instead of enviously. Extremism provokes extremism; provocation engenders counter-provocation; dullness provokes dullness. It's dullness the world is badly in need of – much, much more dullness than we possess. People think we need foreign exchange; export trade; touristic co-existence; utopias; brave new worlds; magic ideologies etc. I believe that we need much more urgently a good supply of dullness. Austria – lucky Austria – is on the right path.

*

The last living representative of the Empire is the heir of the Emperor, Otto Habsburg. He gave up all his claims to the throne of Austria and while he did not explicitly give up his claims to the throne of Hungary, his hopes for a coronation in Budapest in the near future are not bright. I have never met him but I have frequently heard that he is a charming, modest, level-headed and learned man, highly respected and liked even by people who hold no brief for monarchy or the restoration of the Habsburgs.

Years ago I heard a story about Otto which I found not only amusing but very Austrian too. He was in Los Angeles when a friend of mine rang him up at his hotel. It was his Lord Chamberlain who came to the telephone and declared, my friend felt, somewhat haughtily: '*Seine Majestät hat Frühstück in der Apotheke*,' which means: 'His Majesty is having breakfast in the chemist's.' And chemist's, of course, means drug-store.

I couldn't help wondering: if 'His Majesty', why does he eat in the chemist's? And if he eats in the chemist's, why 'His Majesty'?

power and bringing her own diplomacy [illegible] of [illegible] thousand of [illegible] proved [illegible] countries [illegible] much [illegible] foreign [illegible] Admiral [illegible] is on the right [illegible]

The last living representative of the Stuarts is the heir of the [illegible] gave up all his claims to the throne of [illegible] and [illegible] his claims to the throne of [illegible] [illegible]

[illegible]

I can [illegible] Her Majesty [illegible] way [illegible]?

YUGOSLAVIA

ARRIVAL

As soon as you cross the Yugoslav border, south of Klagenfurt, you feel that you have arrived in a poorer country. You felt the same crossing from West Germany into Austria but Yugoslavia is considerably poorer than Austria – and, indeed, Austria is poor only in comparison with Germany. (Austria, unless we improve our performance, is predicted to overtake our standard of living in 1972.) The first thing that strikes you is cars. Austrian cars, you recall, were less impressive, less pompous and less numerous than German cars, but here you descend a further two degrees on the scale. Near the frontier there was not much traffic when I crossed, and a considerable proportion of the cars belonged to tourists. Later on, nearer the towns, the tiny Fiats (assembled in Yugoslavia) became more numerous, and in the towns these cheeky little things – pushing, manoeuvring, obtruding, bustling – dominate the streets. The ubiquitous Volkswagens were even older and more battered than those we met in Austria. Then you see a large number of people on push-bikes. The bikes are status-symbols for many of the riders, proof of newly-acquired affluence; they remain a sign of poverty to us spoiled Westerners.

It started raining soon after I crossed the frontier and the cyclists opened their umbrellas. One thing that will impress you at an early stage in Yugoslavia is the inborn dignity of the people. They are not servile like many Austrians or arrogant like many Germans; not obtrusively chummy like many Americans and not aggressively 'I'm as good as the next chap,' like many Britons. They are people laden with worries and responsibilities, taking life – but not themselves

– seriously. Anywhere else people riding bikes with open red umbrellas in one hand would look as if they belonged to a provincial circus act; here they look sensible, more sensible than men with rolled umbrellas (which they often keep rolled even when it's raining) in the City of London.

Near the frontier I stopped to change money. The transaction was swift, courteous and efficient. No one cared how much foreign currency I was bringing in; the dinar has gained a certain dignity since my last visit – almost the dignity of a man balancing on a bicycle with an open red umbrella in one hand. The café near the frontier post was clean and bright, and the coffee not only cheap, but good. One of the first groups I saw when driving on were some soldiers in shabby uniforms, almost in rags, kicking a brand-new, white football with black spots. One of them kicked the ball into the road, right in front of my car. I had to brake hard not to burst the beautiful white ball. I smiled but no one smiled back.

All the same, the general impression was one of riches and luxury compared with my last sortie into Yugoslavia in 1955. Then, having left busy, noisy, bustling Trieste behind, I crossed the Yugoslav frontier and drove through a cemetery. The silence and the solitude were eerie: I did not see one single car, van or lorry going in either direction until I had nearly reached Opatija. All I saw were one or two peasant carts. The roads were horrible, full of deep holes – with no warning signs – and petrol stations were few and far between. In Rijeka – formerly Fiume, the first town I stopped at – I bought a nauseating lunch which I ate sitting among morose, badly-dressed people while a howling loudspeaker kept repeating a speech Tito had delivered the previous day. I had an advantage: I did not understand a word of it. Not a single person listened although Tito was – and is – popular, but this type of shrieking ballyhoo is always counter-productive. I had been paid a lot of money in Yugoslav currency for the translation rights of some books of mine so I was rich and very keen to buy things. This, however, was a forlorn hope: there was nothing to buy except plum-brandy and a few leather-goods. (I arrived back in England carrying a mini leather-shop: suitcases, brief-cases, wallets, etc., and had to pay more in duty than the sum I had received in Yugoslavia.) I also bought a pair of socks but later they broke. They did not tear, did not get holes in them, did not disintegrate: they broke like a china plate, with a loud crack.

Those days are gone. The streets are cluttered with noisy, cheeky cars, the roads are excellent, petrol stations abound. I reached Ljubljana and asked a man – some official in uniform – where my hotel was. He explained, but added most solicitously that it was madness to pay so much for a hotel-room, it was sheer waste of money – cheaper hotels were just as good. I told him that I had a reservation. He shrugged his shoulders. (The hotel, by the way was excellent and at £3·50 not at all expensive.)

Walking around Ljubljana I found myself in a different world from the Yugoslavia of 1955. Then few people would have dared to dream of going abroad, or of applying for a passport; today travel agencies abound, offering journeys to many foreign lands including Spain and Japan and – even more unimaginable in the early fifties – to Moscow and Leningrad. There are supermarkets, less splendid than those in Manchester or New Orleans, but well-stocked all the same. Girls walk about in maxis and minis. Suits are well made although of poor material. Women's hair-styles are occasionally nearer to Socialist Realism than the latest King's Road craze, but most of the women are well-groomed. There are lots of machines in the shop-windows. In fact, you get the impression that people are slightly gadget-crazy: there are electric razors, hair-driers, toasters, lawn-mowers, the lot. But there are also one or two reminders that you are not in the West: shops are open from 7.30 a.m. till 7 p.m. and even on Saturdays till noon. Breakfast is served in top international luxury hotels from 5 a.m. till 10 a.m. Who the hell, I asked myself, who can afford to stay here, wishes to get up at five in the morning? But I forgot the most important customers: the Germans.

It does not take long to realize that you are where you are: in a country placed fairly and squarely between East and West. People speak freely on most subjects, including Yugoslavia's future after President Tito's death. Yet this subject is taboo in the press. In private human conversations Yugoslavia has a problem to face; officially Marshal Tito is immortal.

WHO IS A YUGOSLAV?

TITO, of course, *is* immortal. He has two great historic achievements to his credit in addition to leading the Partisans in their tremendous struggle: he united Yugoslavia (more or less – as we shall see) and established Titoism. His difficulties in the early days were immense for obvious reasons: there was no such country as Yugoslavia and no such ideology as Titoism.

I am not a very old man but I am slightly older than Yugoslavia. Yugoslavia is not a very old country but she is older than about half of all the other countries of the world. It was said in the old days that if the Austrian Empire had not existed it ought to have been invented. Yugoslavia did not exist and *was* invented. In the Wilsonian era of World War One it seemed an obvious idea that the Southern Slavs (with the exception of the Bulgarians) should be united in one country. But prior to this brain-wave there was no Yugoslav nationalism in the sense there is, say, a Basque nationalism: a desire to become free and to form an independent State. Prior to World War One there were two independent States in today's Yugoslavia: Serbia and Montenegro. Serbia – as well as some other parts of the new country – had been under Turkish occupation for five centuries but the Montenegrins, in their barren, rugged mountains, had resisted even the Turks. At the outbreak of World War One the Slovenes, Croats and Bosnians were ruled by the Austrian–Hungarian Empire, but even within that Empire they were divided: the Croats were under the harsher rule of the Hungarians, the Slovenes and the Bosnians under the Austrians and – as some of my better-informed readers may recall – the war started because the Austrian-Hungarian Crown Prince was assassinated in Sarajevo. The Slovenes are the most westernized and industrialized of all the nations of Yugoslavia, the Croats being the second. These two nations are Catholic. Further south the steeples and spires give way to the onion-shaped domes of the Orthodox Church and to the minarets of Islam. We leave the Western world behind and indeed it was some Slovenes who told me: 'If you want to see the Middle East at its most backward don't cross the Mediterranean; just go to Bosnia.' (This is not quite true; the advice is coloured by a great deal of internecine Yugoslav malice.) The sophisticated, wholly western Slovene university professor is as far away from a semi-illiterate Macedonian donkey-rider as . . . as . . . well, one does not have to go too far in searching for a parallel between North and South: the professor is exactly as far away from the Macedonian donkey-rider as a Milanese banker is from a Sicilian donkey-rider.

'They are not a close-knit family of nations. The sharp cleavage between Serbs and Croats is well-known; it has the appearance of a religious conflict between Roman Catholics and members of the Orthodox Church, but is in reality a savage tribal feud. However, it is not the only national antagonism in this riven country. The Slovenes have an affection for the Serbs, but an extremely chilly attitude towards the Croats. Serbs reply to Slovene overtures with an icy reserve. In the Voivodina, a Hungarian peasant will not speak to his Serbian neighbour. The Serbs never trust a Macedonian. Between Albanians and Montenegrins a blood feud has been raging for centuries. Serb and Bosnian Moslems are kept apart by a sea of blood and tears.'*

Another basic problem was that the various nationalities of Yugoslavia had different and opposite conceptions of what the new State should be. The 1914 war was triggered off by independent Serbia rejecting an Austrian-Hungarian ultimatum. She was overrun by the enemy but emerged

*Ernst Halperin: *The Triumphant Heretic*, Heinemann.

victorious. What could seem more natural to the Serbs than to regard the new State as the fruit of this victory, an aggrandizement of Serbia with the formerly oppressed peoples being grateful for their liberation? And what could seem less natural than this conception to the Croats and Slovenes – let alone to the Montenegrins who had been independent before? The Croats and Slovenes wanted a new Slav State, they insisted on being equal partners and would not dream of accepting Serbian oppression in the place of Austrian oppression. They did not intend to live under a narrow, autocratic, royal dictatorship. To be oppressed by the Karageorgevic instead of the Habsburgs was insufficient progress for them. The position was aggravated by the fact that the Slovenes and Croats had grudgingly accepted Austrian and Hungarian cultural values but looked down upon the Serbs as their inferiors. These racial, linguistic, national, religious and economic differences created disruptive tensions between the wars. These tensions occasionally erupted and the Nazis had an easy task playing them up, dismissing the State and turning Serb against Croat, Macedonian against Serb, Catholic against Orthodox, rich against poor.

That is where Tito came in. During the war he was anxious to unite his Partisans. The Nazis were their chief enemies but not their only ones. Tito was no chauvinist; he was a Communist, a loyal and devoted follower of Stalin. He did not just want a Yugoslavia free of the Germans; he wanted a Communist Yugoslavia. It was quite a tough job for him to fight against both the Germans and the class enemy; national differences had to be eradicated at all costs. Tito promised national self-government to all and vowed that no Yugoslav nation would be allowed to rule, oppress or exploit another.

Tito's post-war Yugoslavia grabbed – well, shall we say gained – some further territories from Italy. She is now the ninth largest state in Europe covering just under a hundred thousand square miles. (To be precise: 98,766 square miles which is equal to 255,804 square kilometres.) She has seven neighbours and is bigger than any of them, with the exception of Italy. (Austria, Hungary, Romania, Bulgaria, Greece and Albania are the smaller ones.) The country – as Tito promised – consists of six autonomous, if not equally advanced and equally prosperous, republics. These are (in alphabetical order): Bosnia-Herzegovina, Croatia, Macedonia, Montenegro, Serbia and Slovenia. Dalmatia, one of the best-known regions, is not an independent republic, but is part of Croatia. Serbia, the largest of the republics, contains two autonomous regions in its territory: the Voivodina – with a Hungarian minority close on a million – and the Kosovo-Metohia region, with almost a million Albanians. Yugoslavia is the eighth most populous country in Europe. In other words Yugoslavia is one of the medium-sized European countries.

Tito's success does not mean that all is well, tranquil and idyllic in Yugoslavia, or that nationalistic and linguistic differences are dead and gone. Far from it. Indeed, I shall have to return to this subject. But it means that Tito is doing his best to keep his promise; that he is as effective in reconciling national and tribal interests as is possible; and being a Croat (and his deputy, Kardelj, being a Slovene), he was more trusted in the early days in this respect than a Serb would have been. In the turmoil after 1918 the foundation stones of Yugoslavia were laid: the State was there, the national sovereignty, the membership of the League of Nations, the national army. But Yugoslavia lacked cohesion: the centrifugal forces seemed stronger than the cohesive, centripetal ones and, at times, members of the armed forces were keener on cutting one another's throats than any enemy's. Ante Pavelić, the Croatian quisling, one of Hitler's more revolting lackeys, massacred as many Serbs as Jews. After the war it was Tito and his friends who turned the State into a nation, the conglomeration of Serbs, Croats, Slovenes, Macedonians, Bosnians, Dalmatians – even Hungarians and Albanians within its frontiers – into Yugoslavs. He deserves full credit: to keep these motley hosts, these warring tribes, these intrigue-loving clans from one another's throats must have been almost as difficult as keeping the peace in a single family, tied together by the bonds of kinship. I wonder if he could have succeeded without the help of his formidable ally, Joseph Stalin? This deceased statesman's contribution to the unification of Yugoslavia may have been accidental; but it was formidable.

Reverting to the opening phrase of this chapter, Tito *physically* is not immortal. The relative peace between nationalities – such as it is – is due mostly to his prestige, authority and the respect he commands. One gathers the strong impression that this is very much the calm before the storm. Would-be successors are positioning themselves for the battle and long knives are being sharpened. The Russians are behind some of the pretenders, anxious and eager to regain their lost influence and to repair Stalin's blunder. One of their most formidable allies is the tension, mistrust and hatred which persists among the various Yugoslav nationalities. Resentments are exploited, mistrust deepened by whispered propaganda, and the flames of hatred are carefully fanned. This is not the only way in which the Russians are following the Nazis' example. If, after Tito's death, a strong man, a real statesman and a pro-Yugoslav gains the upper hand and is able to assert his authority, all will be well; or at least Yugoslavia might be able to weather the inevitable storm. Should Yugoslavia be less lucky in Tito's successor, the Russians have another chance. Force they cannot use: Yugoslavs will always resist force. But fratricidal dissensions might make the Yugoslavs lose what their courage gained in 1948. A similar situation exists in Spain – smiles are on the faces of the courtiers, officers and politicians, an air of perfect courtesy prevails, but daggers and ceremonial swords are already half-drawn. And several thousand miles away Mao Tse Tung is ageing quietly. In the meantime even the most rabid anti-Communist in Yugoslavia prays for the Marshal's life and shouts with true enthusiasm: *Long live Tito!*

TITO – NOT A TITOIST

TITOISM was not born as an idea but as a mishap.

Marxist Communism was conceived as an idea. A German Jew sat down to write a book and less than a century later the Soviet Union was born. Even Yugoslavia was born out of an idea. In the atmosphere of Wilsonian principles people were scratching their heads and trying to find a solution which would include all the Southern Slavs but exclude the Bulgarians who *were* Southern Slavs but had fought on the wrong side. The idea bore fruit, Yugoslavia came into existence.

'Ideology follows the quarrel,' a British diplomat explained to me. How right he was. He was referring to quarrels like those between Henry VIII and the Pope, or between Tito and *his* Pope (to name only two examples out of thousands). The row exploded, the Anglican Church or Anti-Stalinist Yugoslavia was born, and the necessary dogmas were then invented with creditable speed.

Ideology has always been a dirty eight-letter word in Britain, but a sacred cow in all lands under German spiritual influence. The English, discussing general behaviour, speak of *decency* and *honesty* and vague notions of that sort. If rules must be brought in at all, they revert to the rules of sport. If something isn't cricket, it is improper; if it is, it is acceptable. The Germans despise this primitive vagueness and invented the *categorical imperative* as a guide to behaviour. But their clarity is much more nebulous and obscure than our vagueness. Every schoolboy, master, employer, every lover, businessman, politician or jury knows what is and what is not cricket; but who knows what a *categorical imperative* is? Even in the best circumstances it is open to argument and interpretation. And interpretations are as manifold as are the interpreting interests.

The peoples under Germanic cultural influence, however, (and that includes the Russians as well as the Yugoslavs, among quite a few others) insist on the ideology, on the BOOK. The Book is sacred; the dogma is unalterable. If it is no longer any good, a new book has to be written, altering the unalterable and explaining that *the new version is the real orthodoxy.* Lenin changed Marx, always insisting that he was only interpreting him. Thus we got Marxism–Leninism. Stalin went against both – trampled on their ideas and values – and Marxism–Leninism–Stalinism became the new Scriptures. (We had all this with the original Scriptures, too.) We now have the Marxist–Leninist–Maoist version – and many other varieties. Western Communists dismiss Titoists as right-wing deviationists; Chinese Communists dismiss the Russian Marxist–Leninist–Brezhnevists as right-wing deviationists; *double-Maoists* (a sect I met in Sweden) dismiss Mao as a mealy-mouthed, rightist lackey of the imperialists. I, a treble-Maoist, dismiss the double-Maoists as dangerous, Tory-type reactionaries. No one refers to *rights* or *wrongs* – only to the Book (changed out of recognition). Brezhnev occupied Czechoslovakia in 1968 on the grounds that it had deviated from the path of true Socialism. By doing so he retrospectively justified America's Vietnam adventure: the United States interfered because Vietnam had strayed from the path of true Capitalism. The Book – convertible for every possible occasion – is a most useful instrument of Soviet Foreign Policy.

Tito first did what he had to do in the circumstances to prevent his country becoming a Russian satellite like a number of other East and Central European States; then – while preserving the basic Communist structure of his State – did what he thought was best for the economy and the welfare of his people. But such steps, such aims, were just not good enough. *Titoism* as an ideology had to be invented, and even that was not enough. It had to be proved that Tito's heresy was real orthodoxy and that Stalin's orthodoxy was heresy. Or more precisely, that Stalin's version of heresy, hitherto recognized as orthodoxy by Tito, was, in fact, heresy.

*

The Tito–Stalin conflict has been described many times and in great detail. Stalin wanted to rule Yugoslavia as he ruled Uzbekistan or Poland; Tito insisted on being a loyal but independent ally. That was all the difference between them.

There was nothing ideological in it. Tito was in a position to defy Stalin and had done so once during the war when Moscow ordered him to collaborate with Mihailovich. But apart from this one lapse, he was devoted to Stalin and in the early days Yugoslavia was Moscow's most faithful – and, from our point of view – most objectionable satellite. Subsequently, certain political differences developed between Stalin and Tito. Stalin wanted a Balkan Federation without Romania, Tito wanted to include Romania. The Bulgarian Dimitrov first supported Tito then recanted. In spite of this when he unexpectedly died on a visit to Moscow, he was given a grand funeral and became one of the heroes of Communism. Stalin ordered Tito to withdraw his support from the Greek Partisans but Tito – not in the habit of abandoning allies in the same cavalier manner as Stalin – went on supporting the Greeks and, to add insult to injury, reminded Stalin that he had also meant to abandon Mao and had he done so there would have been no victorious Chinese revolution. (Brezhnev probably says today: 'And how wise Stalin was.') In those days a leading part in these Cominform quarrels was played by Zhdanov. Although he was Stalin's most devoted henchman and the loudest of the anti-Tito Brigade, he must have raised the wrong eyebrow at the wrong moment because he, too, died unexpectedly, was given a grand funeral and became one of the heroes of Communism. (Eight years later he was put to further use; it was alleged that he had been killed by Jewish doctors.)

The Yugoslavs reduced the salaries of Russian civil and military advisers to the level of those paid to their own people and Stalin regarded this as a calculated insult (which, probably, it was). The Russians, in turn, claimed credit for Yugoslavia's liberation, while the Yugoslavs took immense – and fully justified – pride in the fact that they had liberated themselves. After all, Churchill had to persuade Stalin to give full support to Tito and a British military mission had already spent a whole year at Tito's headquarters before a Russian mission arrived. The Yugoslavs were very angry when the Russians spoke about the fight of the Partisans in the same breath as the infinitesimal achievements of the Hungarian or Romanian Communist Parties. These were all tactical questions – there was nothing ideological in them. Ideology and counter-ideology were only dragged in after the famous Bucharest resolution of June 1948, expelling Yugoslavia from the Cominform. The quarrel might have been patched up before that but Stalin wanted to teach Tito a lesson. We learn from Khrushchev's book* that Stalin remarked that he would only have to lift his little finger and Tito would collapse. He lifted his little finger, lifted all ten of his fingers, lifted and shook his fist, howled, got purple in the face, but Tito grew stronger and stronger.

Thus the merits and demerits, the rights and wrongs, of the quarrel are unimportant; but the fact that there has been a quarrel is of the utmost significance. Those people who care about such things have been debating for centuries – and will go on debating for further centuries – whether Martin Luther was right or wrong. Most of us care very little about the subtler points of theology but it is of the utmost importance to all of us that there *was* a Martin Luther; that he did quarrel with the Pope; and that he, too, invented a religion to back up his quarrel.

It is easy to see the historic significance of the Yugoslav quarrel. Stalin's defeat at the hand of Tito was the end of the monolithic Empire; for the first time it was made clear

* *Khrushchev Remembers*, André Deutsch.

that there was more than one road to Socialism, and Khrushchev's Belgrade visit in 1955 underlined this. It also ended the most exciting chapter of the quarrel. The outbreak of the Korean War in 1950 rang the alarm bell: it showed that the Russians *might* use force against those who opposed them. Their failure in Korea dispelled this fear but it was only Khrushchev's visit in 1955 which told the Yugoslavs, in so many words, that they might now feel safe. Tito had triumphed – but every triumph has its price.

There are no victors in modern wars: so runs the fashionable saying. The reference is usually to Great Britain, who is in a worse position than some of her defeated enemies. I feel it would be fairer to say that Britain has paid a terrific price for standing alone for a while in the struggle to save the free world. We often forget that victory is not always disastrous; that one of the victors, the Soviet Union, does enjoy the full benefit of victory. On the other hand, she could cope with her enemies but not with her allies. Tito was the first to strike a blow; then came many others – East Germany, Poland, Hungary, and most important of all, China (Tito made Mao possible, and deserves more gratitude from the latter than he receives). As long as the Soviet Union has many allies, her enemies have little to fear.

*

Every man's character and even his fate is formed by his relationship with his parents and (I have referred to this earlier) every Central European State's character and fate has been formed by its relationship with the Soviet Union. The Soviet Union is the father of modern Yugoslavia. Tito is a devoted Communist; he grew up full of respect for Stalin and his land; his people were taught to utter the Great Man's name with the utmost reverence. Then from one day to the next – for the people of Yugoslavia knew nothing about the difficulties within the Cominform – the loyal son was banished from the parental house. Tito was called a hyena, a traitor and an American agent. In response, the Yugoslav press spoke feebly and with apparent embarrassment about the equal rights of all Socialist States. Then they slowly began to criticize certain bureaucratic abuses in Russia – still a far cry from criticizing Stalin himself. We witnessed a pitiful farce in August 1948 – a few weeks after the stunning blow of expulsion – at the Danube Conference in Belgrade. The Yugoslavs were cut dead and treated with utter contempt in their own capital by the Soviet delegation and its other satellites, yet they voted faithfully with the Eastern bloc and demonstrated their loyalty to the very people who were calling them imperialist spies and chained dogs. They voted against the Western Power's participation in the Danube Commission – an act they may regret today.

Tito's first problem was that of many sons who are driven to hate their fathers: *he resembled his Old Man*. He was always a much more civilized person than Stalin, but he was not a gentle flower by any means. He lacked Stalin's brutality, but he was the son of the system; Yugoslavia was a minor Soviet Union. And no one can totally eliminate his inherited character-traits. In Yugoslavia, even today, a small group holds power: Yugoslavia is still a totalitarian dictatorship even if a comparatively mild one; the Communist Party plays more or less the same part as in other Communist States, even if it has a different name; the Workers' Councils (more of them later) are only seemingly democratic: the majority do decide but the majority are under pressure as to what to decide. And we still have the unanimity, the dull speeches, the dull press, the sycophancy, the whole paraphernalia of the Soviet system: Stalin was always – after the shocked silence of the first few weeks – denounced in strictly Stalinist terms. Heretics have to recant in the same repulsive manner as in Russia. Tito's triumph was almost complete when Khrushchev came to see him and was humiliated by him at the airport; (this was not planned; Khrushchev said some silly things in his speech). Yet, this triumph must have been a mixed blessing. No one likes to kick his former idol; no one really likes to humiliate his father and spit in his face in front of his own children. And Daddy was still powerful; Daddy was rich; Daddy did not forget. His successor may have asked for forgiveness but even he will never forgive Tito for the very fact that he was made to apologize. And the last chapter of this quarrel has not been written yet. It will be written after Tito's death.

Tito emerged as a grand international figure after 1948. In some important aspects he outdid two other statesmen who held the stage at different times: de Gaulle and Dubcek.

Churchill used to say about de Gaulle, during the war, that of all the crosses he had to bear, the Cross of Lorraine was the heaviest. De Gaulle's assertions of his independence were masterly, but a bit hard to bear. Similarly, Tito played his hand audaciously. He had the Yugoslav army re-equipped by the Americans, absolutely free of charge. In return he conceded no bases, signed no treaties, made no significant concessions and admitted no foreign military missions to the country. He took all available military and economic aid from various Western Powers and it was he who dictated the terms. He out-de Gaulled de Gaulle.

Dubcek, at a later period, spoke loudly – and quite superfluously – about 'Communism with a human face'. The face of Tito's Communism is a shade less human than Dubcek's would have been but it is much more human than Russia's. And here lies another of Tito's great achievements.

THREE STEPS TO THE RIGHT

TODAY, according to most observers, three main types of Communism face the Capitalist system. There is, first of all, the Soviet system which still occupies the dominating position; Mao Tse Tung is on the left, Tito on the right. And we, the so-called Capitalists, are on the other side of the fence. According to one observer* it would be more to the point to say that three types of capitalist-bureaucratic system – our own, Soviet Communism and Titoism, face the Communist system which is genuinely represented by Mao alone. Of course this is a deliberate simplification. (*Oversimplification* is a silly, derogatory word rarely used in its proper sense; *simplification* is a blessing, it makes ideas clearer and easier to grasp.) Our capitalist system has many shades, the US system differs from the Dutch, the Japanese from the Portuguese; the Soviet system, too, has ceased to be monolithic and Hungary differs from the Ukraine and East Germany from Romania. Finally, Mao also has his Titos. All the same, the above classification remains essentially true: Communism, and let us speak for a moment of the Soviet type only, has drawn much closer to Capitalism than either of the two parties cares to admit – just as there is very little to choose between modern Toryism and Harold Wilson's Socialism.

Whenever such statements are made, they are greeted with an uproar, or with condescending, superior and knowing smiles, or with impatient, dismissive waves of the hand. Nevertheless, they remain true. Before the 1970 British elections innumerable articles explained how silly this

*George Mikes – a Hungarian-born Briton.

contention was, the commentators pointing out the vast and unbridgeable differences between Tories and Socialists. But no articles were needed in 1972 to explain that the French Terror differed from the rule of Louis the Sixteenth, or in AD 63 emphasizing that Christianity was not identical with the old religion of Rome; and even in 1917 it was pretty obvious that the new Russian system differed from the régime of Tsar Nicholas the Second. The very fact that so many commentators wasted so many words in 1970 pointing out the differences between the parties is proof that these differences were so slight that they had to be pointed out. The trouble is that words remain the same but their meaning changes. We still speak, for example, of the struggles of Trade Unions against exploitation, as if we lived in another age. Of course all is not well; of course workers still have legitimate aspirations; of course employers would still exploit workers if they could. But they cannot. Today the Trade Unions are the most privileged class in the country – privileged to break the law. They often hold the public to ransom to achieve their sectional interests while their more romantic supporters, glowing with honest indignation, shout nineteenth-century slogans and look rather pathetic. We have the spectacle (in 1971) of the Labour Party bitterly opposing an industrial relations bill which they had meant to introduce themselves but failed to bring off. No verbiage or noise can conceal the fact that both parties were aiming at the same broad result. And when the broad aims of the parties are the same, when the Tories are committed to the Welfare State and the Socialists are driven to fight the Trade Unions, what is left of the differences? Nuances, of course; and the vested interests of the parties: after all neither organization is likely to declare itself superfluous and go into liquidation. And – extremely important – there are two different party organizations and two different sets of people claiming office and power.

And if Conservatism and Socialism have been drawing nearer each other *within* individual states, the same has happened *between* states too. Modern capitalism would seem anathema to most nineteenth-century economists; small enterprises still belong to individuals but the large are public companies and the individual shareholder has no power whatsoever in the running of a company; he is a complete nonentity. Heavy taxation has made vast inroads into private wealth, death duties make the passing on of vast fortunes almost impossible; under the beneficial pressure of Socialism, we have established the Welfare State, and even in countries where the expression 'welfare state' is regarded with horror, the state helps the individual in a manner which would have been unimaginable a century ago. On the other side of the barricade, in Eastern Europe, there are also small enterprises in private hands; the individual – the 'workers', and 'people', to whom *all* enterprises are supposed to belong – have even less say in their running than capitalist shareholders; and great differences in wealth are just as apparent there as they are here. 'Proletarian millionaires' existed in the Soviet Union in the thirties and the gap between rich and poor is more appalling in Russia than it is in Portugal, or Venezuela. We, over here, say that the Stock Exchange and the rat race are essential; they, over there, maintain that Marxism–Leninism – as expendable as the Bible – is sacrosanct. It is only the Chinese who are trying – not very successfully at the moment – to establish something truly different. But even this attempt at being truly different – if we recall the late twenties in the Soviet Union – has a distressing air of *déjà-vu*.

There is a kind of state-bureaucracy which calls itself Capitalist and another kind of state-bureaucracy which calls itself Communist. They differ from each other just sufficiently to be at each other's throat but the real clash is the old-fashioned nationalistic rivalry between great powers – the same as divided Elizabeth of England from Philip of Spain, or the Hittites from the Phrygians.

A reasonably intelligent adult is interested in two aspects of a 'system', whatever the label attached to it may be: general welfare and freedom. He will insist that no human being should live in penury and will desire a fair amount of freedom for the individual in order that the arts may flourish and – more important still – a change of régime may be possible without a bloodbath. Capitalism in itself guarantees nothing: people can be miserably poor under it (*vide* India), and as heavily oppressed as they were in Nazi Germany; can be, and are, in a number of capitalist states today. But in capitalist states people *can* be reasonably well-off and *can be* comparatively free. Capitalism is, at least, not incompatible with freedom. The US and Britain are not ideal societies – far from it – but life is much better, even for the violent protester or above all for him, than in Spain, Guinea or Albania. A short while ago I heard in the same news bulletin that a family with five children had been evicted in London – thrown on to the street – because they could not pay an extra five shillings weekly rent to the Council, and that a Velasquez portrait was sold for well over £2,000,000. In the inevitable television interview the evicted father said that five shillings (25p or 60 cents) was a *huge sum*; the buyer of the Velasquez declared that the picture was *comparatively cheap*. There is something basically rotten in a system which makes such discrepancies possible. Neither can we hope for *any* system which will bring the essential improvements quickly. Improvements in human conditions have always been slow and gradual and have always brought their own, unexpected and inevitable new problems in their wake. But – as I have pointed out – in our not too attractive system a fair amount of economic justice *may be*, at least, coupled with a modicum of freedom.

The Soviet Communist experience, on the other hand, is disheartening. A minority rules the state and freedom is an unimaginable luxury. No minority government can afford freedom because a free vote would sweep that minority government away. The dictatorship of the proletariat has always been the dictatorship of a bunch of bureaucrats, justified in the name of economic justice and progress. The Communists are, in fact, justified in claiming certain successes. The feudal slaves of Hungary, for example, have disappeared and the worst kind of poverty has been eliminated. There are no more barefooted peasants. Nevertheless, in most countries, Communism as an economic system is a disastrous failure; people live badly, have neither freedom nor consumer goods, neither rights nor hard currency. Mao is far away – in Central Asia, not in Central Europe – so I shall forget about him. But I have had to point out what I have just said about the opposing European systems in order to make my main point clear: Yugoslavia, calling itself a Communist State, is a true bridge between Capitalist state-bureaucracy and Communist state-bureaucracy. It has deviated from the Russian system without embracing the Western one. It is a half-way house. It is undeniable that it is a better, happier, freer and richer country than the Soviet Union or any of its satellites; and it is also undeniable that *every improvement was accompanied by a step to the right* – in the direction of the Western system. Let us examine, briefly, the three main steps to the right.

*

Tito decentralized his economy as much as he could and introduced Workers' Self-Management throughout industry and, indeed, throughout the life of Yugoslavia. A great deal has been written about this experiment, by hostile pens as well as by propagandists, but the gist of it is extremely simple.

In the Soviet system a factory has a *norm* – it has to produce, say, 100,000 barrels a year. If it produces only 90,000 barrels it has failed, the manager is sacked or declared a saboteur. (Not long ago he was shot as an enemy of the people or an enemy agent.) If the factory, on the other hand, produces 110,000 barrels, all is well, laudatory speeches are made, glowing articles written in the press, the workers are extolled as heroes of Socialism and the manager gets the Communist equivalent of a knighthood. No one cares if the barrels are so inferior that they fall to bits in a month and flood the cellars with wine or vinegar. No one cares whether 100,000 barrels are really needed. Distribution is another company's job and another manager's worry. Never mind if there is an over-production of barrels while there is an agonizing shortage of packing cases – which the same factory could put right. As long as they produce their 100,000 barrels a year, all is well and everybody is happy (except those people who get inferior barrels instead of superior packing cases which is what they really need). The most highly paid people in any Communist enterprise are the political Commissars (under more modern names) and party watch-dogs.

The Yugoslavs had the original and world-shaking (but very un-Leninistic and even more un-Stalinistic) idea of relating production to consumption. They made the barrel factory self-sufficient. It is still under public ownership and no private, capitalist exploiter has yet appeared on the scene. But if there is no need for 100,000 barrels, they will have to produce packing cases instead; if they produce shabby goods, these will be returned to *them* (and not to a distributing company, unknown to them). If the factory is doing well and earns a lot of money, salaries and wages go up – everybody gets his share of the surplus; if they are doing badly, everybody earns less. If the factory keeps losing money it *may* be saved by the State but it may not, in which case it may go bankrupt in the old-fashioned capitalist way. Political informers and party-men are eliminated as useless – so it is an added beauty of the scheme that the only people to make money are those who work hard and deserve it. The enterprise is run by Workers' Councils, elected by all the workers; and directors (their equivalent of a board) can be dismissed by the Council; at the same time no ordinary worker may be sacked without the Council's knowledge and approval.

Production plans, marketing and other problems are decided by the board, and major steps by all the workers. Enterprises can go into liquidation; they can change their line of business; they can amalgamate. Socialist takeover bids are as hotly debated as Capitalist ones, except that shares do not go up and down because there are no shares.

All that is needed is that the general meetings of the interested companies – in other words a majority of *all* the workers and officials concerned – should express their desire to pool their resources and agree on the details. This sounds like absolute democracy but it is not. The directors have a decisive say and they are often under political pressure from above as to what to say. Nevertheless, an ordinary Yugoslav worker has as much – and more – say in the running of his enterprise as a capitalist shareholder has in the running of a public company.

The question of nationalism which bedevils so many issues in Yugoslavia is, of course, felt in industry. In some industries *size* is a decisive factor: the larger the better. Yet Yugoslavia has (to take one example) two petrol-refinery systems – a Serbian and a Croatian – which compete with each other like mad all over the country: even in Serbia and Croatia. There is no hope of their uniting; indeed, it is much more likely that Slovene, Bosnian and Montenegrin petrol companies will come into existence; after all, national rights are sacred. Similarly, it is difficult to appoint the best men to all the important posts. As in Austria during the Coalition, where a Socialist had to be replaced by a Socialist and a member of the People's Party by another member of the People's Party, so in Yugoslavia a Serb *must* be replaced by a Serb even if a Croat would be twice as efficient. (Before I cause an uproar, I hasten to add that you can permutate and vary the names of nationalities in any way you please.)

The Russians condemn this system but they, of course, have a vested interest in its failure. Some Westerners praise it but emphasize that it has not gone far enough. The truth is that it is suffering from some obvious teething troubles and is still far from perfect. Orthodox Communism is older, yet it does not work so well; orthodox Capitalism is a few millenia older still and pretty objectionable in many ways, too; the Yugoslavs are experimenting with something new which works. It creaks, it groans, it jerks – but it works, and it is being improved all the time as it goes on. Yugoslav enterprises – all State-owned – are involved in advertising campaigns, compete with one another and often litigate against one another. The Yugoslav worker cannot be content to fulfil a norm laid down in a faraway central office and he cannot shrug his shoulders if the goods produced in his factory are shoddy; he cannot strike light-heartedly either. Strikes are unlawful but a Yugoslav strike would not be a simple blackmailing exercise against the public or a weak – or mean – employer, but a blow to the workers' own pocket. So the system does work: people, on the whole, are satisfied and proud of having invented something new and intelligent. The system, indeed, works better and better as time passes. The rate of growth is good (inflation, too, is as rapid as in the more advanced countries). The Yugoslavs are succeeding because they took over those elements of Socialism which are beneficial – there is no exploitation, no capitalist owner – and because some clever chaps among them thought of this staggering new notion, called *profit*. To work for profit – to want more and more money – is extremely un-Leninistic but it seems to be extremely human. Just one of those human failings we must acknowledge with a rueful sigh.

*

Another ingenious and original discovery made by Tito's men was that not all foreigners are spies; and even if they are, it does not matter. There is little to spy on nowadays. All great – and small – powers know one another's main secrets in any case, so what does it matter if a few hundred thousand spies or potential spies arrive in one's country to ferret out minor secrets, so long as they bring in a lot of money? In other words, Yugoslavia was the first Communist country to discover tourism; and is today – deservedly – one of the leading tourist countries in Europe.

The country is very beautiful. It is excellently situated as one of the nearest – and certainly one of the cheapest – Mediterranean lands. It has blue seas, lovely beaches, enchanting islands, rugged coasts. Graceful Venetian buildings abound, as do numerous spas and mineral springs, while in the forbidding Karst region, limestone rocks and plenty of caves are thrown in for good measure. Caves have an irresistible fascination for many people and Yugoslavia is very rich in deep, dark caves. Khrushchev wrote that he had regarded the Crimea as unsurpassably beautiful but when he saw the Dalmatian coast, he felt humbled. Some of the regions are a trifle overdeveloped – the beaches at Dubrovnik in August look like the pavement in front of C & A's in Oxford Street just before the doors are opened for the January Sales. Other regions are hopelessly underdeveloped. The Yugoslavs build, develop and learn; by now they know how to run their hotels although occasionally you hit a blank. I found the leading international hotel in Zagreb pretty awful. It is American – and so are its prices. Innumerable page-boys in colourful uniforms turn revolving doors for you, beautiful chandeliers hang from the ceilings and you sink knee-deep into the carpets. But there is no air-conditioning and Zagreb can be very hot and you feel that the price *should* include air-conditioning. The rooms are spacious and the armchairs lush. There was a huge television set in my room which did not work; I had a truly lovely bathroom with a lot of pink porcelain and the water was always hot except in the morning; the telephone was out of order and a revoltingly poor and insipid breakfast cost as much as a wonderful English one at Claridges. The room was a heat-box placed in the middle of a marshalling yard – goods-trains passed almost at the bottom of my bed and – Yugoslavia being a booming country – heavy goods traffic was lively.

This hotel was an exception; most Yugoslav hotels are adequate and reasonably cheap although prices are rising rapidly and you realize that there must be moments in a budding tourist industry when prices run ahead of service. The Yugoslavs seem to have a penchant for building their really expensive hotels near marshalling yards. I slept almost on the railway lines in Belgrade's best hotel too (otherwise an excellent establishment). I was told that (a) the other side of the building was completely quiet and (b) the railway station was going to be removed in a year or two. A reassuring thought, but small comfort for a man who wishes to sleep on this side of the building, this year.

Tourism has worked miracles for Yugoslavia. It brings in hundreds of millions of dollars every year and it is one of the most important industries in the country. Dalmatia used to be one of the most poverty-stricken areas of the land; today it is one of the richest. Yugoslavia has her problems: tourism requires vast investments and gives only seasonal employment to many people – yet it has proved a major blessing. In a sense, Tito swopped Stalinist orthodoxy for capitalist tourists and has no reasons for regretting the exchange.

Tourism is, by the way, one of the miracles of our age. It can solve all the economic problems of the world. According to an old and unkind saying the inhabitants of certain Eastern lands live by pinching one another's washing. Scientists explained that this was economically impossible. But scientists were, once again, wrong. This method – tourism shows – is perfectly feasible. Post-war affluence may be on the wane but the package-tour is flourishing. People go to Yugoslavia but the Yugoslavs, too, go abroad in increasing numbers. It seems that it does not really matter how rich people are: as long as even penniless people keep visiting one another's countries, they can keep one another rich. This is actually the Mikes Law of Economic Growth: *overall poverty – if properly husbanded – can produce overall wealth.*

*

About Tito's third step to the right all the satellites still speak with condescension. It was indeed a step of despair and Tito had to swallow his pride to take it. I am speaking of his decision to allow Yugoslav workers to go abroad, first to Germany and Switzerland. 'For a Communist country to allow this to happen ...' a high-ranking Hungarian official told me, shaking his head. Having said that much he fell silent as if words had failed him. A Communist country, apparently, must keep its workers at home in penury, and disguise the fact that there is unemployment in the country. Still less can a true, orthodox Communist country allow frontiers to be crossed freely and reports to be circulated that the wicked capitalists have a much higher standard of living.

But Tito, having been born under a lucky star and having been excommunicated from the Cominform, allowed the unspeakable to happen and this act of despair did more good to Yugoslav economy than most carefully planned and thought-out policies.

As workers left Serbia and Croatia, Bosnians and Macedonians came to fill their places. In other words, just as some Yugoslavs emigrated to wealthier neighbourhoods, people from the poorer parts of Yugoslavia started moving into the richer areas (still poor enough to send many of their own men abroad). This inner migration is hardly ever mentioned. The great economic gap between the various Yugoslav republics is a sore point and no one likes to talk much about it. This exodus of workers eased the unemployment situation – and this is the first beneficial result of Tito's decision.

Less obvious ones followed. The Yugoslavs are much liked abroad and create a great deal of good-will for Yugoslavs in Germany, Switzerland and Austria etc. They are not resented, like many other foreigners, because people know that they will eventually go home. As I remarked before, it is easier to get a good Yugoslav dinner in Munich than a good Bavarian one. Whenever you see a large German car in a tiny Yugoslav village – off the beaten track – you may rest assured that it belongs to no German tourist but to a Yugoslav plumber, waiter, restaurateur or factory-worker on a temporary visit from Zürich or Düsseldorf. And – here comes the main point – these Yugoslavs abroad keep sending home good, hard currency which enriches their country enormously. Foreign tourists in Yugoslavia are one of the largest sources of currency;

but Yugoslavs living abroad surpass them. *Yugoslav workers abroad bring in more money than tourism* – and that is saying a lot. Many expatriates return home in large cars, not only as visitors but to stay: they open shops or hotels, buy land and enjoy a much higher standard of living than before, thanks to their foreign adventure.

Tito may have moved to the right according to the Marxist Bible, but he emerges triumphant. His country is a Communist country and he still accepts the Creed. But he has added a few maxims about the Capitalists to those of Lenin:

1. If you can't beat them, join them.
2. Any Communist country needs capital much more than any capitalist countries need Communism.
3. The aim of any true proletarian revolution is to get rid of proletarians – by making them well-off.

*

The main purpose of the Yugoslav experiment is to supply evidence that democracy is possible without political parties. The thesis is far from proven yet; Tito is trying to square the circle and has put up a pretty good show so far.

Yet, in some respects he fails to notice that he is succeeding too well.

Timing is one of the most important factors in all human achievement. Today's outstanding success might have become a flop yesterday and could be a failure tomorrow. Today's virtue might have been a crime last week and may well become one again next week. In the McCarthy era brave and honest Americans – who opposed Hitler long before America entered the war – were persecuted as 'premature anti-fascists'. Or let us return to Yugoslavia. Take the case of Andrija Hebrang and Streten Zujović. These two (I give only the bare outline of their complicated stories) opposed, before the break with the Cominform, Yugoslavia's utterly unrealistic, megalomaniac Five Year Plan. They were imprisoned as saboteurs. Zujović was set free after some years – after the break, of course – and rehabilitated with apologies; but Hebrang died in prison. Everyone acknowledges now that the two men said the right thing; but they said it too soon. They were premature Titoists.

Milovan Djilas is another victim because of being ahead of his time. A hero of the Partisan war, a former Vice-President of the State, a former intimate friend of Tito's and one of the most brilliant brains in Yugoslavia, he is in and out of prison for – among other things – his outspoken criticism of the régime. Once he was ready to humiliate himself and recant his so-called crimes but his integrity proved too strong: he could not live with a lie and he had to profess his real views. Whether Djilas is right or wrong is beside the point: he is a natural product of Titoism. He sensed and understood the essentially good elements of Titoism and acted upon them; he realized that if Titoism was not incompatible with dictatorship, it was at least *compatible with democracy*.

He spoke out; but spoke too soon. A premature democrat. A Djilas would be utterly unimaginable in the Soviet Union or East Germany. He is no enemy of Tito; he is one of the glories of Titoism. Let us hope that he will prove a Zujović, not a Hebrang.

HOW TO BECOME NON-ALIGNED

'IDEOLOGY follows the quarrel.' This dictum is valid for foreign affairs too. After the break of 1948, Tito was angry and determined but also bewildered and puzzled. His old friends turned their backs on him and spat venom into his face – although this was difficult to do with their backs turned. Tito could not possibly turn to the West – not so soon, anyway – and thus prove correct the allegations that he was an imperialist agent, spy and hyena. So, for a while, he vacillated between the two groups and was at a loose end.

This vacillation eventually became a policy; it was given a name, raised to the rank of an ideology, and strict and noble rules of the game were formulated.

The name found was *non-alignment*. Yugoslavia's primary aim in those difficult days, in which she succeeded, was, of course, to preserve her independence. The simple idea, at the beginning, was not to be committed to either of the two large power-groups. But later, when the climate changed in Yugoslavia's favour and both sides began to court her, it became obvious that there was much more to this non-alignment than met the eye.

The main rules are these:

1. Non-alignment is not only a policy but a livelihood. With a little skill and cleverness – and Tito has plenty of both these qualities – you can make a good living at it.

2. You behave like an old-fashioned, coquettish yet virtuous French lady of the 1890s: you wink, you smile, you close your eyes with a passionate sigh, you look

unattainable, you look attainable, you show your knees occasionally but you never go to bed with anyone. Or only very, very seldom.

3. In every given dispute you take liberties with your friends and not with your opponents. Your friends cannot let you down or allow you to go over to the other side; but if you give hope to your opponents (smile coquettishly, show your knees, etc.) they will go to considerable lengths to soften you up, trying to win you over.

4. Non-alignment means many things. A Yugoslav diplomat complained bitterly to me about the cynicism of the world: 'People always doubt our pure intentions and suspect that we are playing at power politics.' On the evidence of the world's past history, pure intentions and unselfishness in foreign affairs cannot be taken for granted, so people's cynicism is perhaps forgivable.

5. All non-aligned powers are non-aligned but some are more non-aligned than others. Some are nearer to one power-group, others to another power-group. Quite a few feel safer non-aligned if they are safely aligned.

6. Although non-alignment means many things it hardly ever means non-alignment. Some countries (Algeria, for example) give what they call a *radical* interpretation to the notion. The non-alignment of this group means that they give all possible support to the liberation struggle of ex-colonial lands. To put it a shade more clearly, their non-alignment is just another word for alignment.

7. Yugoslavia's own non-alignment means that she, too, was involved in the Middle Eastern struggle on Nasser's side. Tito felt deep personal attachment and admiration for Nasser – they had too much in common not to admire each other. There is nothing you can admire more in another man than your own greatness. This peculiar interpretation of Middle Eastern non-alignment was explained to me by one of Yugoslavia's chief non-alignment experts: 'We had to make an exception here, because we are against Russian expansion in these regions,' he said.

I blinked, I made sure that I got him right, then said:

'But surely, if you are against Russian expansion you ought to oppose their pro-Arab policy which gives them more influence, more bases, more colonial ascendancy in the Mediterranean. In this case you ought to support Israel.'

He smiled a superior smile, suggesting: it is amazing how naïve some laymen can be: 'Not at all. We believe the longer the struggle lasts, the more the Russians will gain by it. Our interest is that the struggle should end as soon as possible.'

That makes it clear. Non-alignment, in this particular case, means not only that you help your opponent to achieve his aims, but help him to achieve them fast.

This muddle and confusion should convince everyone that the non-alignment policy works splendidly. Yugoslavia's foreign affairs are in good order. Russia was – and is – her main problem. Their relationship has fluctuated. After Stalin's mad fury we saw Khrushchev's Canossa visit. The Hungarian Revolution shook Tito at first: he did not like the spectacle of a Communist régime being deposed by a popular uprising. But still less did he like the spectacle of the Russians interfering with tanks to quell a Tito-like deviation. This is Tito's worst fear and that is why the Russian occupation of Czechoslovakia in 1968 was a terrible shock which created new tensions and suspicions between the two countries. Nothing could be more abhorrent to Tito than the Brezhnev doctrine which tries to justify Russian military occupation in cases where a country deviates from Russian orthodoxy; which, in fact, denies the possibility of various ways to Socialism. Yugoslavs were afraid that the Russians might seize the opportunity to cross *their* frontiers too in 1968. In that case the Yugoslavs would have resisted with force. They would have been defeated but the Soviet armies would have faced prolonged and determined partisan warfare – showing to the world that the Russians were the true, legitimate successors of the Nazis. Or an air attack – perhaps on Sarajevo – might have triggered off a new world war.

In the event, the Russians did not invade Yugoslavia;

but their move on Czechoslovakia had wide repercussions in those regions. Yugoslavia drew nearer to Romania – another Communist country with an independent, often anti-Russian foreign policy. Romania, to a small extent, is also a non-aligned country. Although a Russian satellite, she, too, is trying to maintain the balance between the *three* power-groups: she welcomed President Nixon in Bucharest and endeavours to remain friendly with Mao. Albania, too, was terrified of a possible Russian invasion and she is trying to bury the hatchet and tone down the shrill voices raised *vis-à-vis* Yugoslavia. An improvement of relations with Albania means an improvement with China. Tito's relationship with Italy – once an irreconcilable enemy because of Trieste and Istria – is excellent. Yugoslavia is also on good terms with Hungary and with the West. She rejoices over East–West *rapprochement* and is pleased if, say, West Germany and Poland get on – as long as they do not get on too well, in which case Yugoslavia's non-alignment loses a great deal of its significance.

Yugoslavia, with her non-alignment, was a lone wolf at the end of the forties. But today non-alignment has grown into a world movement: a motley crowd comprising more than half of the members of the United Nations. They are a new force; a new alignment. Some say a new power-block. They have their conferences and they try to bring their views into harmony. The charge that they are trying to form a power-block may be unfair: they have no military strength and their organization is even looser than that of the British Commonwealth. There is little danger that the non-aligned will exert pressure on the great power-groups and establish a tyranny of the non-aligned over the rest of us. But they protest a little too much about not seeking power. They do seek influence and influence is power. I am ready to believe, however – with some hesitation – that this power might be used for a good purpose.

ARE WE FUNNY?

'ARE we funny?' the Professor asked me, walking along the charming baroque streets of old Ljubljana. He taught something very complicated at Ljubljana University, connected with technology, and was a serious man. He threw a side-glance at me as we walked and his voice sounded anxious and – although he was a mild and gentle man – slightly aggressive.

'I am not quite sure what you mean, Professor,' I said cautiously. 'Who are *we*?'

'Are we, the Yugoslavs, funny as a nation?'

'Oh no,' I replied politely. 'Of course not.'

He walked beside me in thoughtful silence for a short time.

'Then you must be disappointed in us,' he said apologetically.

'Of course not. First of all I have not come here to draw a cartoon. Secondly I have seen a lot of amusing things, all the same.'

'A lot of amusing things, yes,' and by now he sounded worried, 'but, you say that as a nation we are not funny.'

'No. As a nation you are not funny.'

I stopped to admire a beautiful wrought-iron gate with a charming courtyard behind it but the Professor – who hitherto had pointed out every remarkable brick – was not interested.

'The Germans, would you say, are funnier?'

'Much.'

'And the Italians?'

'You can't really compare them.'

'And the Greeks? Would you say even the Greeks are funnier?'

I did not wish to sound too cruel: 'No. I should say the Greeks are about as funny as the Yugoslavs.'

'Not *less* funny?' he asked hopefully.

'No. No less, no more,' and my voice sounded unusually firm and final.

We walked on to see a few more of the graceful houses, churches, gates and courtyards – he reverted to his rôle of conscientious and knowledgeable guide – then he led me into a garden. We passed a number of impressive statues – fearful figures with martial faces – and reached some small round tables, charmingly decorated with flowers. We sat down and ordered some bilberry-juice, which he insisted on paying for.

'Do you know,' he asked as soon as the purple liquid arrived, 'that Serbian and Croatian are practically one and the same language? Serbian is written in the Cyrillic alphabet – having been under the influence of the Orthodox Church for centuries – and Croatian is written in the Roman alphabet. There are slight differences, of course – but very slight differences only. So small, in fact, that *some* Croatian dialects are closer to Serbian than to literary Croatian.'

'Yes,' I nodded vaguely because I had no idea what he was driving at.

'Yet all attempts to unify these two languages have always failed. Worse than that – Serbian *and* Croatian used to be called Serbo-Croat for a long time. But the Croats will have none of that any more. In Croat regions the language is called Croato-Serbian nowadays.'

'Yes,' said I even more vaguely than before.

'Isn't *that* funny?' he asked me triumphantly.

'Most amusing,' I agreed without true warmth. Then as an afterthought: 'And what about *your* language, Slovene?'

'Ours is an independent Slavonic tongue,' he replied with lofty disdain, 'nothing to do either with Serbo-Croat or Croato-Serbian.'

I found *his* attitude funny but could not politely say so.

'Do you understand the Macedonian question?' he asked.

As no living – or, for that matter, dead – person understands or has ever understood the Macedonian question, I could not claim to be the first exception.

'The Macedonians are divided among three countries. The Bulgarians claim them to be pure Bulgarians and say their language is a Bulgarian dialect; we maintain that they are a Yugoslav nation; the Greek colonels – and all Greek governments – insist that they are Greeks of Slav descent.'

'I have travelled in Macedonia and I know,' I told him, 'that the Macedonians who aspire to nationhood – and quite rightly so – find absolutely nothing funny in this situation.'

'The Macedonians are notorious for not having any sense of humour.'

They are a proud, brave, ferocious yet kind and generous people; they are also poor and backward and perhaps a strong sense of humour is not among their most conspicuous characteristics. Neither do they find it particularly funny that the trouble-makers of the Kremlin, whenever they wish to warn or blackmail Yugoslavia, encourage their Bulgarian satellites to raise the Macedonian issue.

The Professor looked at me, then continued: 'Do you know,' he went on, 'that Yugoslavia has *two* alphabets, *three* religions, *four* languages, *five* nationalities and *six* republics?'

'But I also know that, in spite of all, she manages to remain *one* country,' I replied.

'You speak like Tito,' he said impatiently. Then, probably thinking that he had gone too far, he demoted me: 'Or at least like Kardelj.'

'I accept Kardelj,' I told him. 'He is a Slovene like yourself.'

He sipped a little more purple juice.

'Do you realize that even the newly discovered institution of the *week-end* has become a national issue and gives rise to misgivings? Croatians – who have cars, and that's quite a lot – come over to us in Slovenia because Slovenia is much more beautiful than Croatia.'

'What about Dalmatia?' I interrupted.

'Dalmatia is Dalmatia, even if it belongs to the Croatian Republic. Besides, Dalmatia is too far to go for a week-end. So they come over to us and that hurts the pride of many Croatians. They say that our women are more beautiful, much pleasanter and more liberal.'

'But isn't this – like so many other problems – an economic question? They are simply annoyed that their money is spent over here? That good Croatian dinars are exported to Slovenia?'

'Perhaps,' said the Professor. 'But we can't help it if our country is lovelier and our women are more beautiful.'

'That's all very well,' I told him now, feeling he should not have all his own way, 'but isn't it true there are 92,000 Slovenes living in Zagreb while very few Croats come over to settle here? For week-ends, yes; but to live here – no. Indeed is it not true that 10,000 Slovenes still move to Zagreb every year and that the *Slovene* population of Croatia grows more every year than the *total* population of Slovenia?'

'Oh yes, that is true.'

'And isn't it also true that a six-mile stretch of the new main motorway being constructed between Croatia and Austria-Steiermark shows no sign of being finished? The Slovenes – I am told – refuse to finish it, because this road would reduce the importance of the present main road which runs through Slovenia. And you want people and goods from Austria to come through Ljubljana – not directly into Croatia? Is *that* true?'

'Most assuredly.'

'And isn't it also true,' I asked, 'that Croatian regiments will have to be used to complete this road because the Slovene government have proved themselves past masters of procrastination? What do you say to that, Professor?'

He sighed: 'I say to you that you have completely missed my point. I wasn't trying to prove that we Slovenes are better than others. The whole point is that we are just as bad. This conversation has been conducted mainly on a Slovene–Croat level because I happen to be more familiar with these problems. But you can discuss these matters from any other angle – Bosnians and Macedonians are just as bad, Montenegrins and Albanians are worse and Serbs and Croats are, of course, the worst of all. All I am asking you is: have you heard of any other country, any other State, consisting of several nationalities who all dislike one another?'

'Have *you* heard, Professor, of a country called the United Kingdom? Have you ever heard of the great love of the Scots for the English? Or the adoration of the Welsh for the English? Or the Irish for the lot?'

'United Kingdom?' he murmured. 'That's Britain.'

'Call it that,' I agreed reluctantly, as I have always been a pedant.

'And would you say that even the *British* are funnier than we?'

'Incomparably funnier.'

He took out a cigarette and lit it, his first the whole afternoon.

'I know we are a small nation,' he said thoughtfully, 'a not very important nation; perhaps we don't have too many great heroes; perhaps we lack many of the most dazzling virtues; I know we are poor. But we *are* funny.'

I shook my head firmly.

'You are a great nation in more ways than one. Your post-war history made you extremely important. Your President is one of the heroes of these decades. You are endowed with great virtues: you are brave, imaginative, fiercely independent yet very tolerant. You are growing richer. But funny you are not.'

He sat there, puffing at his cigarette a long time, then he said: 'Do not send me a copy of your book.'

I promised not to.

FIERCE TOLERANCE

In spite of the diversity within the State, there is one national characteristic which distinguishes Yugoslavs from all other nations. Or more precisely: not one national characteristic, but a strange combination of two seemingly incompatible traits: a fierce love of independence with an amazing degree of tolerance.

Both characteristics could be traced back to this or that nationality in Yugoslavia and explained through its history and traditions. But it is fair to say that by now both the love of independence and the tolerance have become Yugoslav – as opposed to Serbian or Croatian, etc. The famous tolerance occasionally creaks, almost bursts at the seams and threatens to explode. Nevertheless, in spite of these trials and stresses, the statement remains generally true.

The Yugoslav is fiercely independent, first of all, on the individual level. You cannot order him about: he is not servile, not anxious to please; neither is he arrogant or self-assertive. He carries no chip on his shoulder – just regards himself as a human being like anyone else. He prefers to use his own judgement. I would not go so far as to say that a Yugoslav waiter *never* brings you what you have ordered. Sometimes he does. But often he uses his own judgement – purely in your interest – and brings what he deems to be good for you.

Many officials are not in their offices when you call: it would be incompatible with their fierce love of independence to sit in one dingy room all day. I chased one or two officials for days in vain, and was told by their colleagues that they must be out. So much I had guessed myself. It was said courteously but nothing was added to it. No apology; no excuse; no vague suggestions that the officials might be back in five minutes or five hours. They were out; they were fiercely individualistic Yugoslavs and they chose to be out.

This fierce independence – you feel – goes a shade too far on occasion and in small matters. But small matters are always symptomatic of big ones. The air-conditioning in my Belgrade hotel-room broke down and I reported this to the concierge. He told me that I would be moved to another room – from 416 to 520. I wanted to move my things but he said that everything would be done for me. All I had to do was to go to the new room when I returned to the hotel. I memorized my new room number – 520 – but he, most obligingly, wrote it down for me on a little card. On my return, late at night, I found none of my things in room 520. To make matters more interesting, I could not find them in 416 either. They were found next morning: the luggage porter had decided to keep them for the night. Purely in my interest. He deemed it safer. He was a fiercely independent Yugoslav and acted on his own judgement. When he heard that I had to do without my pyjamas and toothbrush, he laughed aloud and found the matter amusing. After this move – from 416 to 520 – I received no messages, no mail, no telephone calls for five days. No one could reach me and people complained that although we had made fixed telephone-appointments I was not available in my room at those times. I, on the other hand, complained that I had been sitting in my room, waiting for the calls which never came. It turned out eventually that the receptionist had never registered my move so that all my letters went to room 416 and all my telephone calls were put through to that room which – as the air-conditioning had broken down – remained empty. But the receptionist – I was given to understand – was a fiercely independent Yugoslav and he found it incompatible with his national honour and human dignity to make little scribbles on small pieces of paper just because I had changed rooms.

This love of independence manifests itself on more serious

and important levels, too. Before the war Yugoslavia was one of the most backward states in Europe. The Communists have changed this to a large extent but it was only in 1952 that agriculture ceased to be the most important branch of the economy. After the war Yugoslavia – modelling itself on Russia – declared that 'the land belongs to those who till it'. This means, in Russian terms, that the land is taken away from those who till it and the peasants are forced into collectives. Collectives have failed everywhere (remember Stalin's purges, Khrushchev's disastrous difficulties, a series of failures in all the satellite states, etc.) and Yugoslavia was no exception. The Yugoslav peasants resented this regimentation more fiercely – and more successfully – than others and today only fifteen per cent of the land belongs to collectives; the rest – more than two and a half million holdings – is cultivated by individual peasants.

It would be too much to say that Yugoslavia, as she claims, has solved her agricultural problems. No land and no system – Communist, Capitalist, Fascist, Syndicalist, Henry-George-ist or Anarchist – will ever satisfy farmers or peasants. For them it is never the right system, never the right subsidies, never the just policy, never the right crops, never the right prices, never the right weather, never the right God. But Yugoslav peasants are perhaps as satisfied as peasants can be expected to be. And even if the methods of cultivation are a little backward, the country gets the food it needs and can export some of its foodstuffs, its plum-brandy, its wine. There is, however, one very black spot here: the aged and incapacitated peasant does not get any sort of pension or state-aid which is a major scandal in a Socialist – or any other – State.

Communist regimentation does not work with unfailing precision in industry either. Up to five people can be employed by small enterprises and this number is to be raised to ten. It may well be imagined that people often prefer to remain independent and work for themselves. Several hundred thousands of people are privately employed and – here the Yugoslav tolerance comes in – the state does not discourage them. The government knows that certain services are better performed by individuals or small firms. Their fierce love of independence manifests itself, above all, in their mutual, brotherly detestation of one another. Serbs suspect and dislike Croats and vice versa; Bosnians are always ready to fight almost anyone; Montenegrins – no softies by any standard – are also the targets of many jokes. And so on, indefinitely. But should any stranger or outsider try to interfere, Yugoslavia becomes one united nation, facing and defying the whole world if need be. No one will dictate to them; no one will tell them how to run their affairs; no more than a patron in a restaurant will *order* a waiter about. The Russians learnt their lesson in 1948. During the tension between Yugoslavia and the Cominform, Russia used incessant blackmail. Russian tanks were concentrated and carrying out 'exercises' on the Yugoslav border, first in Hungary, then in Bulgaria, then in Romania. Yugoslav tanks – few though they were in number and prone to break down – were always there to meet them. And if there were no tanks available, artillery and infantry were waiting for the Russians. Stalin knew that had he tried to invade Yugoslavia, he would have met with armed resistance. Brezhnev knew the same twenty years later. After the occupation of Czechoslovakia tremendous excitement shook the Balkans for a day or two: would the Russians – people asked – live up to the full fatuity of the Brezhnev doctrine that Russia was entitled to use force to preserve what she called Socialism, and use this excuse to settle accounts with Romanian intransigence and even with Tito? The Yugoslavs, once again, were ready to fight. I am not criticizing the Czechs for not provoking a bloodbath and plunging – who knows? – the world into a new war. I am only registering the fact that they did not resist while the Yugoslavs were ready to fight. They were always ready. They will fight Russians, Chinese, Americans – anyone.

Titoism is essentially the expression of this fierce love of Yugoslav independence, based on the success of the Partisan war which in itself was the outcome of the same ferocious determination (helped by a suitable terrain).

Yet the Yugoslavs' hot temper, their head-strong determination, their flaming passions are strangely compatible with wise moderation and tolerance. This is a unique combination. There are many violent nations and tribes in this world (take almost the whole continent of Africa from the Arabs, through the new, black republics to South Africa) but they do not know what tolerance means; or else take the tolerant British or Dutch, who although they cherish their freedom as much as anyone, can hardly be described as fierce, boisterous or ebullient.

I noticed how decent the Yugoslavs were to their Hungarian minorities. Much more decent than the Hungarians used to be to Croats before 1914 and incomparably more decent than the Romanians are to the Hungarians today. Towns have their own old Hungarian names. The Hungarian name for Novi Sad was *Ujvidek* and the name is freely used in private and in public, in speech and in print. 'Well, that's the Hungarian name for it,' the Serbs say and would not dream of protesting against it any more than the Austrians would when the English call their capital Vienna instead of Wien. Or the Italians against our calling Firenze, Florence. But try to use the old name of *Kolozsvar* instead of Chuj and the Romanians will regard it as something approaching high treason. There is an old Hungarian war memorial in Osijek, commemorating soldiers who died fighting *against Yugoslavia*, and it has been left standing. The Hungarian and Albanian flags may be freely used alongside the Yugoslav. All the many nationalities in the Voivodina – even small groups like the Slovaks or Romanians – are allowed to cultivate their own language and to have their own newspapers. Sartre – some of my Hungarian friends proudly pointed out to me – was published in Novi Sad in Hungarian but was banned in Hungary. This goes for many other authors. Yugoslav tolerance occasionally produces ludicrous results. Many Hungarian peasants treat their Serbian neighbours with impatience verging on contempt; they were there before the Serbs they state, still regard them as intruders and refuse to learn their language. The Serbs, they say, should learn Hungarian if they want to talk to them. And they do. Hungarian is one of the recognized, official languages of the region of Voivodina and any Serbian official who has dealings with the public must learn Hungarian. In the Voivodina Assembly – parliament – every speech is translated simultaneously into *five* other languages, making six languages altogether. Voivodina beats the United Nations hands down.

During the war the Croat Ustashis perpetrated acts of revolting cruelty against the Serbs on a staggering scale. The barbarity of these massacres horrified even the SS – not a squeamish lot. But there is little recrimination on the part of the Serbs. The unforgivable is forgiven – or at least, not held against a whole nation. There *is* antagonism between Serbs and Croats, based on clashing economic interests, on tradition, on national rivalry: but there is no blood feud.

All this does not amount to the picture of a Paradise. The political police are not ubiquitous; people are not dragged out of their beds and sent to prison arbitrarily; they are not afraid to speak their minds. But the political police are there in the background and even if they do not cripple the life of the country they cast a shadow. People can and do criticize their rulers – federal and local – and this criticism is often outspoken and vociferous. The press is freer and less dull than in Russia or in the satellite countries. But there are no opposition parties and no one would be allowed to advocate the return to Capitalism. You cannot criticize the Head of State either, but issues in which Tito is involved and about which he has spoken can be openly discussed and Tito's views may be contradicted. There is no censorship. Independent ministers often come under fire and the Federal Prime Minister was not long ago attacked in a way which would do credit to any old-type democracy. If someone oversteps the permitted boundaries, the law steps in. There are no show-trials and no one is forced to confess to crimes he has not committed. But the word *law* can be misleading. After all, the Nuremburg laws were also laws; the law of the Soviet Union which meted out heavy punishment to the relatives of defectors to the West *even if they knew nothing of the person's intentions*, was also law. I only mean to point out that the law can be oppressive, brutal, immoral, repulsive – indeed, illegal. To speak of trials and invoke the law is meaningless; it all depends on the fairness of the trial and the decency of the law. There is no country in the world with an absolutely clean record in this respect. Yugoslavia fares reasonably well, but it is a great pity that its Stalinist origin is in evidence here and there and that Milovan Djilas and Mihajlov are still in and out of prison because instead of just praising and shouting hosannas to Yugoslavia's new freedom they dared to use it.

NOVI SAD

THE government of the autonomous province of Voivodina – just south of the Hungarian border – invited me to be their guest for a few days. The Voivodina is part of the Republic of Serbia, occupying one quarter of it. It has its own provincial Assembly, Executive Council and Administration and a population of about two millions. I stayed in an old Austrian-Hungarian fortress – today a tourist hotel – in Petrovaradin, just outside Novi Sad, and enjoyed every minute of it. I was in Yugoslavia – the most advanced, the most progressive and happiest Communist country in the world; but I also found myself back in pre-World War One Hungary, the Hungary of 1905 or so – a world I knew well from novels and memoirs. (It is most enjoyable to travel backwards in Time; it gives you the impression that the fleeting moment can be captured and perpetuated, after all.) This was the Bacska – the homeland of the poet Kosztolanyi – the rich, indolent, sleepy Bacska. It was couldn't-care-less land, the home of good food, provincial conceit and unsurpassable wisdom. Because what can be wiser than to be satisfied with your lot and enjoy life? Not as it could be, not as it might be – just as it is.

I was getting keyed up for my homeland, Hungary. If the Bacska, this miniature Hungary with its 700,000 Magyars, was so pleasant, how much pleasanter the real thing must be. I was amused to notice a great deal of condescension towards Hungary. The Hungarian-language newspaper published in Novi Sad was, I was told, not only better informed and freer but also larger in size than anything published in Hungary. I was also told that *everyone* in Hungary was reading *Magyar Szo*, the paper in question. Once I discussed some international question with journalists on that paper and they made some good points. I agreed with them and said the London *Times* had made the same points. The foreign editor's face turned serious and he said: 'Then they must have taken it from us.' In other words not only was everyone in Hungary reading *Magyar Szo* but even *The Times* leader-writers were studying it (in Hungarian) before committing themselves on major issues.

The Hungarians of the Bacska, as I have said, feel smug towards Hungary. Certainly Budapest is the great centre of Hungarian culture; certainly the theatre of Budapest is magnificent. A few points like that are conceded. But Hungary is a Russian satellite; food is poorer than in the Bacska; people more oppressed and worse off. They are spoken of as poor relations – a far cry from pre-war irredentism. And what amused me most, the Hungarians from Voivodina keep going over to Hungary for shopping and for holidays – because Hungary is cheap for them, the dinar being a stronger currency than the forint (which, in turn, has also improved since tourism started in Hungary). The Hungarian intellectuals and professionals of the Bacska (not the peasants though), to my genuine surprise, were proud of being Yugoslavs; they were also proud of being Magyars. They lived in the best of all possible worlds. Novi Sad – it was pointed out to me – used to be a small town of 30,000 people. Today it is a thriving city of a quarter of a million. Life was nowhere pleasanter than in Novi Sad; the best food was in Novi Sad, better than in the Provence; a great many famous people were born there; and they had a bridge over the Danube which was unique in one respect. (I cannot recall that one respect – it is highly technical – but everyone is aware of it in Novi Sad.) The Hungarians' pride exceeds local-patriotic chest-beating. They are proud of being citizens of Yugoslavia and enjoying equal rights with other nationalities. They bicker with others – as everybody bickers with everybody else – but they have the full right of bickering. They have their own press, radio and television station, their own schools, dance-groups and orchestras. They call Novi Sad the Serbian Athens. Not the Hungarian but the Serbian Athens (a reference, by the way, to Pericles and not to Colonel Papadopoulos).

I was amused. Amused, but also impressed and delighted. Forty-eight hours in Novi Sad and I felt an irresistible longing for Hungary. Then, soon afterwards, forty-eight hours in Hungary and I felt an irresistible longing for Novi Sad.

CZECHOSLOVAKIA

CLANG!

THE Hungarians were to chuck me out. The Czechs refused to let me in.

HUNGARY

ALIEN'S RETURN

'WHAT do you feel? What is it like to be back in the old country?'

The question was asked by my travelling companion.

'I can't really tell you,' I replied. 'I feel nothing in particular but then my emotional reactions are rather slow.'

Having had to abandon the idea of visiting Czechoslovakia we had left Novi Sad, driven through Subotica – Szabadka, for me, the town of Kosztolanyi,* the poet – bought petrol at the last Yugoslav filling station where everybody talked Hungarian and crossed the frontier at Horgos, a village near Szeged, which was once Hungary's second largest town but slipped to fifth place (with its slightly more than 100,000 inhabitants) when the Tito controversy cut off the Yugoslav hinterland. I had the same painful feeling I had experienced when crossing from Germany into Austria and from Austria into Yugoslavia: once again I was entering a poorer country. Everything – the town of Szeged as well as the villages – was shabby, crumbling, filthy; people were badly dressed and looked tired and overworked. A lot of people were working in the fields. I knew that the living standard of the Hungarians had improved in certain respects, yet these pathetic figures, mostly women, were bent double, toiling hard with their bare hands. The peasant may not be a feudal serf in Hungary any more – indeed he is doing rather well – but today this sort of work is done with machines not only in

*I have left off the little dots and dashes deliberately because most non-Hungarian readers find them disturbing. Apologies to my Hungarian readers.

California but even in Northern Yugoslavia. These Hungarian women lacked even primitive tools. It became even more depressing when we reached the outskirts of Budapest. It was not merely that the houses were grimy, or sometimes disgustingly filthy, but an eerie feeling of gloom, of Kafkaesque disintegration, was overhanging the place. I had crossed the Hungarian border with romantic anticipation; now I felt angry and hurt. This was a personal insult.

*

I left Hungary in 1938, during the Munich crisis. Originally I had been sent to London for a few weeks as a newspaper correspondent but I have stayed ever since. This was my fourth visit to my homeland since those pre-war days.

During the war I worked for the Hungarian Service of the BBC and was regarded by the Hungarian semi-fascist (and later fully Nazi) authorities as a renegade and a traitor. After the Liberation I was treated as a noble creature, a true patriot who had helped the Allied cause and thus also the cause of the glorious Soviet Union. As I went on working for the BBC for a number of years I soon became a renegade and a traitor once more, and a hyena into the bargain – the fashionable epithet for anyone who criticized a People's Democracy. (I quite like hyenas. They are characterful creatures, if not pretty. Also, I believe it is more decent to feed on dead bodies than to kill happy, living creatures for your lunch. But I understood that when I was called one it was not meant as a compliment.)

In my pre-hyena days (February 1948) I returned to Budapest to visit my parents. I am one of those rare creatures who love their parents (they are, alas, both dead now) and I was keen to see them again. My step-father was a doctor whom I had not seen since my departure in 1938; my mother had come to London in 1946 and I had also met her a little later in New York where she was staying with my brother. My step-father refused to leave Hungary – a feasible proposition in those early days – so my mother returned to Budapest, via London. It was then that I promised an early visit home which had become overdue. I had married a few weeks earlier, but I had no money to pay for my wife's ticket. So I decided to go alone. My wife said that this was to be our honeymoon and she would like to join me, a not unreasonable wish under the circumstances. In the end she borrowed the money from her mother. Our marriage broke up several years ago for reasons which form no part of this narrative. But perhaps it did not augur well for the future that I wanted to go on my honeymoon without her. If I may leave one word of advice to the male half of humanity – a final word of wisdom on honeymoons – always take your bride with you.

Budapest was a Paradise in February 1948. Or near enough to Paradise. Britain had just passed through a horrible, shivering winter, with a fuel crisis and rationing of all sorts. We in Britain were all ill-clad, cold and hungry, still feeling the strains and privations of a long war in our nerves, brains and bodies. The only way to fly to Budapest in those days was *via* Prague and the time-table was so fixed that the plane for Budapest left Prague half an hour before the plane for London arrived, so travellers had to spend twenty-four hours in Prague. One way of boosting tourism. But as my sister had just fled from Hungary and was in the Czech capital, I meant to spend a few days there in any case. Prague was much worse off than London. Everything was rationed and hardly anything was available even on ration-cards, which I did not possess in any case. There was no coffee, no sugar, no milk, not enough bread – there was nothing. There were in fact only two commodities you could buy without ration-cards: hats and spats. I needed neither; but as I needed spats even less than hats, and as one feels a compulsion to buy *something* in a city where nothing is available, I did buy a hat. (A few weeks later I left it under a seat of a theatre in London. That was my last hat ever.) From hungry, miserable, ill-tempered, morose Prague I arrived in Budapest – a place out of this world. It was elegant, gay and full of optimism. Political parties were functioning, the coalition seemed to work, the newspapers were free, lively and critical, and people were full of hope and optimism. But what hit the eye even before one could examine the political situation, was the wealth. Rationing did not exist; you could buy white bread, boxes of the best chocolates, suits, shoes, black-market nylon stockings – even hats and spats. The coffee-houses – still in full bloom – were packed and people were sitting over steaming aromatic cups of coffee covered with whipped cream, eating rich, chocolatey cream-cakes the like of which the poor Londoner had not seen for years.

This dream-like period would be short, of course: the Communist Party had already suggested to the Social Democrats that the two parties should 'unite'. This, to put it more clearly, meant that the Communists had already opened wide their jaws ready to swallow up the Socialists – one of the first steps towards turning Hungary into a dreary, odious Stalinist concentration camp with the hangman the busiest Stakhanovite. Historically Hungary's *dolce vita* lasted for a moment; but *this* was the moment and I enjoyed it. My visit was a private one – I came as a son, not as a journalist. I saw my parents, cousins, relations, friends, colleagues, drank a lot of steaming coffee with whipped cream on top, enjoyed again the half-forgotten taste of food on which I had been brought up, the only food I really like – paprika-sausages, fried chicken, peasant ham – and was delighted. I left Hungary full of pleasant memories, but not without a grave foreboding about the shape of things to come. This had nothing to do with my being clairvoyant. I have always been a lousy prophet, because I have always expected everything to turn out well. But in this case it was impossible not to perceive the gathering storm.

My parents left Budapest – with ordinary, legal passports – early in 1956 and, having spent a few weeks with me in London went to settle in the United States. In October that year, the Hungarian Revolution broke out and the *Panorama* programme of BBC Television sent me to Hungary to make a film. I had left the BBC Hungarian

Section years before but I remembered only too well that whenever I had introduced myself as coming from the Hungarian Service of the BBC, the invariable response was: 'Good God, I never knew the BBC had a Hungarian Service!'

On this occasion, when I arrived on the border, I told the frontier guard my name and he asked: 'Mr Mikes, from London Radio?'

He was impressed and this suited me. I had no Hungarian visa – I depended on his good-will. After some difficulty, I succeeded in convincing him that he ought to let me in. Once this was achieved, I had to tell him that I was not alone: he had to let in – without visas, of course – a crew of four other people, representing BBC Television. The policeman looked at me with astonishment: 'Good God, I never knew that the BBC had a Television Service, too.' For him the BBC consisted of the Hungarian Service only.

The events of those days are described in another book of mine* as well as in about five hundred books by diverse hands.

Seven years passed and the Hungarian Minister in London invited me to go and see him. He did not exactly invite me to go to Hungary but suggested that if I decided to go, I would be *persona grata*. I was flabbergasted. I asked him if he had seen my *Panorama* film and read my book. He smiled and assured me that neither the film nor the book had escaped the attention of the Hungarian authorities. And still I would be welcome? Yes, very much so. (Hungary was after tourists and was also keen on presenting a new, more civilized face to the world: if a dangerous, anti-régime man, an author of a book on the '56 Revolution, was welcome, Hungary was obviously a safe country for everyone to visit.)

A few months later, in May 1964, I went to Budapest to write a long article for *Encounter*.† I shall give one or two

* *The Hungarian Revolution*, André Deutsch.

† See September 1964 issue.

short extracts from that article without referring to it again. Quite a few things said then are still valid. It began:

'We are poor. We have nothing, except our high standard of living. We live about three times as well as we can afford. This is the real *Wirtschaftswunder.*' It was the manager of a State enterprise who spoke. 'It was easy for the Germans,' he continued, 'they have raw materials. They have the Ruhr. They work like hell. What's so miraculous about rebuilding a country with outside help, natural riches and hard work? Look at us. We have absolutely nothing to boast of, no one helped us – on the contrary – and we didn't really work. Yes, sir, this is the real economic miracle.'

And so the article went on, full of affection for charming, witty, insolent Budapest. It was a loving and lyrical piece, about the joy, humour and ebullience of a city I loved.

Then a typical Hungarian reaction followed. While my bitter, angry, critical book on the Hungarian Revolution produced an official invitation to visit the country, my rhapsody created such offence that my application for a visa was nearly refused six years later. I failed to understand this until I heard – in Budapest, on this last visit – that my references to the decay and the dirt of the buildings had caused offence. 'You may differ from us in your political views,' one of the very high-ups told me, 'but if you say that we are dirty, that we don't wash and that we stink, then we take offence.' I had said nothing of the kind, I protested; I had only mentioned the crumbling, broken-down buildings which today – after another six years of disintegration – look even worse.

I wrote in 1964: 'I was watching Budapest and knew that Budapest – or at least a section of it – was watching me, its prodigal son who had now returned with a British passport in his pocket and some outlandish ideas in his head. I must not be caught up, I told myself, in a web of emotions. I could not, of course, judge this city as I could judge Beirut or Vladivostok, but I must try to keep a level head. Nor must I blame Budapest – I told myself – because I could not possibly find what I am really in search of: my youth.

I knew all along my route that I was not only driving eastwards in space but also backwards in time. I wanted to meet that slender youth with thick, fairish hair who used to dwell here, but that youth had disappeared – with his silhouette and, indeed, most of his hair – and had become the past. This, if I want to be fair, is not the blame of Budapest, not even of Rákosi.'

Now – driving northwards from Szeged, in 1970 – I meant to be even more cautious because I was aware of even greater pitfalls. I did not want to be trapped by emotion. But I was six years older; I hated the idea of the ageing author re-visiting his birthplace and being nostalgic about it; furthermore, I was doing another programme for BBC Television – *One Pair of Eyes* this time – and needed all my wits and all my so-called objectivity. My companion's question: 'What is it like to be back in the old country?' still rang in my ears not only as a gentle inquiry – which it was – but also as a dark warning. Driving along the roads, looking at the Great Plains – the flat, dull countryside – I knew I was lost. I was too deeply involved with this bit of Europe. It was no good pretending that I had just arrived at the venue of the last chapter of my book on Central Europe; that I was just a BBC reporter doing a customary job; that I was a foreign correspondent who happened to know the language. The BBC knew perfectly well why they had sent me to Hungary and not to Bulgaria. I loved this country; I love the language; I love the poetry; I love my friends. I respect Keats and Shelley and Eliot but for me poetry is – and will always be – Ady, Babits, Kosztolanyi and Gyula Juhasz; I shall always add up figures in Hungarian; I shall always dream in Hungarian. My very English life is only superimposed on Hungarian foundations – within the English writer I have become by some odd quirk of fate, there lives a small Hungarian boy, murmuring ancient lines of Hungarian poetry and watching me with irritated, quizzical eyes. I knew I would not be able to write about this country as I would about Afghanistan or Ecuador.

And that is why the dirt and the neglect of the place upset me so much. I felt that they had allowed *my* countryside to go to rot; *my* villages to crumble; *my* people to go on living a primitive life bending double in the fields, working with their bare hands and growing prematurely old; they had allowed *my* suburbs of Budapest to disintegrate. Oh yes, I knew that I was crossing one of the poorer regions of the country; but the Great Plains formed, after all, two thirds of the whole – and if two thirds of something is poor, the whole is poor. I knew that I was driving into Budapest from the wrong direction. I knew you gathered a better impression – both of the countryside and of the city – if you came in from Vienna. But that was a Potemkin aspect. That was all cosmetics; *this* was the country's real face. I was in a towering rage by the time I reached the inner parts of Budapest, the offices of IBUSZ, the official Hungarian Travel Bureau.

I had left London months before but I had introduced Michael Houldey – the producer of my BBC film – to the London representative of Ibusz. Houldey asked the London man to book us all into the hotel on Margaret Island. The Ibusz man – a smooth operator, oozing genuine, unadulterated Central European charm – promised everything most obligingly. When we arrived in Budapest months later we had no rooms. Not only no rooms on the Island but no rooms anywhere. No rooms at all. No one had heard about our pending arrival. And Budapest was full – there were no rooms available. They were very sorry. When eventually we landed in the Royal Hotel – an old, pompous, uncomfortable and ridiculously expensive establishment – we were received with cool reserve by some of the officials and breezy familiarity by others, the latter group being absolutely determined to be funny and live up to the gay reputation of Budapest.

In Kabul I would have shaken my head in mild amusement. Here I was outraged. And I suddenly remembered an account a friend of mine had given me of *his* journey to Budapest. It had puzzled me then. He is a lecturer at one of the English universities, an able young man who left Hungary in 1956 and went back for the first time to visit his old mother. He gave me a report a few days before my own departure.

'I was delighted to see my mother. It really made me happy. The city is lovely. People were kind and helpful. The girls are lovely and most obliging. I had the time of my life. Food was delicious – Hungarian dishes have no rivals. I enjoyed seeing my old friends. I even loved the gipsy music.'

'But what was your general impression?' I asked him. 'What was it like as a *whole*?'

He looked at me with surprise and non-comprehension. 'Bloody awful, of course.'

Now I began to understand what he meant.

BUT FOR THE GRACE OF GOD . . .

I WAS keen to check up on some old memories. We were always told, when young, that Budapest was one of the most beautiful cities in the world. Shortly before my departure in 1938 I was trying to persuade a friend – a Jew and a fighting liberal and anti-German – to leave the country before it was too late. We were crossing the Chain Bridge, the Danube flowing beneath, the Buda hills studded with millions of tiny lights. He looked around and said: 'I can't leave. Budapest is the most beautiful city in the world.'

'Have you ever been abroad?' I asked.

'Never.'

'Not even as far as Vienna?'

'Never.'

'Then how do you know?'

'Look around. I know. Nothing can possibly surpass the Danube.'

He stayed and was shot dead by Arrow Cross (Nazi) hooligans, and his body was thrown into the beautiful Danube.

Yes, I too remembered the sight as very beautiful. But was it? Having seen Rio de Janeiro, Hong Kong and Istanbul in the meantime – would I still find Budapest beautiful?

Well, the city reminds me of one of those wonderfully preserved middle-aged ladies who look beautiful at a distance. Look down from the hills of Buda at the famous view, with the Danube bridges, the Parliament building,

Margaret Island, the surrounding hills, Fisherman's Bastion and the Coronation Church, and – Istanbul or no Istanbul – you will enjoy one of the loveliest sights in Europe. The dilapidated, crumbling and decaying buildings down below are the good lady's wrinkles and the bags under her eyes. You do not see them any more than you see the many new buildings, the spacious, well-built workers' homes with day nurseries for children, where people live with constant hot-water but terribly overcrowded.

An old friend will wink at you: 'Well, what do you think of the women of Budapest?'

You wink back roguishly and keep the truth to yourself: that while you have seen a number of pretty girls – where do you not? – you do not have the feeling that you are in a city of ravishing beauties, as the legend tries to maintain.

I was, of course, more than thirty years older than when I left this city originally; perhaps not *every* woman is a beauty in my eyes any more. But every other woman still is. If the women of Budapest have become less alluring, it is because their clothes are made of third-rate material and they have much less time to spend in front of the mirror. No shame to them – on the contrary; I am simply recording the fact that you do not feel any more, as you did between the wars, that you are in a city of languid, breath-taking beauties. Clothing is expensive in Budapest and wages are pretty low. It is true that women are better dressed than they were six years ago – minis, midis and maxis abound and the whole atmosphere is more with-it than before; there is more sex and less Party ideology in the air – but there is still a crying need for large, efficient department stores selling well-cut, even elegant, clothes at reasonable prices. With Marx and Lenin they are well supplied; it's Marks and Spencer they need.

I kept telling myself that I liked it there, that I was happy to be back, but I could not help noticing that I grew more and more irritated. People were gossipy and the words 'in confidence' had no meaning; they all had malicious tongues and humiliating one another under the guise of leg-pulling was a national pastime. But there were two things in particular which got on my nerves.

First, their boastfulness. It is quite in order to point out the good things and the improvements to a visitor, and there are, in all fairness, quite a lot of achievements to be proud of. But talk to anyone and he will tell you that Budapest is the most beautiful city in the world; that their women are the loveliest; that their country is the best, at least among the satellites (which is perfectly true); that they are the happiest, gayest and most likeable people, a race unique under the sun. Among themselves they grumble, and this they can now do without fear of the political police. The Right to Grumble is one of the few important basic rights they have gained for themselves under Kadar. But as soon as an outsider appears the mood changes. And I was more often than not regarded as a foreign observer, not as a son of their city. (They were quite right to suspect me, of course.) Local patriotism I suppose, is one of the strong, primitive forces of the human soul, and most people of Budapest have turned propagandists for their city. I mentioned after my last visit that even former revolutionaries had tried to convince me that all was well. When I reminded one of the three years he had spent in goal, he replied with a broad grin: 'But do you know how much better the food is in a Hungarian prison than in an average English restaurant?' (No, I did not know. But I do know that food has improved out of all recognition in the average English restaurants, so perhaps it has done the same in the average Hungarian gaol.)

After a week or two in Hungary I understood the mechanism of this gay – or rather, desperate – boasting much better. I shall revert to politics later, but to understand the Hungary of the seventies, you must keep one thing in mind: the 1956 Revolt was the Hungarians' last, desperate attempt to get rid of the Russians. Not of Communism but of the Russians. Soviet guns and tanks gave a decisive and final answer to this attempt on 4 November 1956. No one in Hungary is likely to forget it;

if anyone was inclined to forget it, the invasion of Czechoslovakia in 1968 was a clear reminder: the Russians are there to stay. Hungary was under the Turks for one hundred and fifty years; under the Austrians for about two hundred and fifty years; she might as well settle down for a century or two of Soviet domination and make the best of it. And that's exactly what Hungarians are doing: making the best of it. They are paying lip-service to things and ideas Russian; they appear to be – and perhaps many of them are – good Socialists; yet they do their best to remain a civilized Central European nation which has not gone over to the East; which has not returned to the steppes of Mongolia. People boasting about the wonderful conditions in Hungary were not trying to impress me, but to reassure themselves. They were not really boasting; they were whistling in the dark.

The second thing that got on my nerves was their wit. About three quarters of the Hungarians I met had to be witty – inexorably and mercilessly witty – all the time. You could hardly get a straight, relaxed answer from anyone. They *had* to be amusing, charming, lighthearted and super-clever. Breezy badinage and cheap irony fill the air. It is a terrible effort – joints creak badly all the time. How often did I feel: 'One more attempt at wit and I'll strangle you!'

I visited one of the political potentates who kept regaling me with *bon mots* of Kadar's. When he was asked to permit Rakosi – the exiled tyrant who died in February 1971 – to return from the Soviet Union, he flatly refused. Some of his colleagues tried to prevail upon him to change his mind and to let the seventy-nine-year-old man come back, not as an active political force, of course, but as an old-age pensioner. 'You cannot pension off a powder-keg,' Kadar replied. 'Dynamite remains dynamite, even if you pay it a pension.'

It is only Kadar in the whole country, I was told, who has the sense and courage, when a problem of the past re-emerges to say: 'Let's see how Horthy tried to solve it.' For lesser men Horthy's very name is anathema. The year of my visit, 1970, was also the year of the centenary of Lenin's birth and the whole country – when speaking in an official voice – made awe-struck and sanctimonious utterances accordingly. It was only Kadar who remarked: 'I don't know what Lenin would do today if he were alive. But I am certain of one thing: he would not study his own old writings day and night and would not try to solve all the problems of the present on the basis of his own, outmoded ideas.'

Or again: when Kadar travels – to make a speech in a country town for example – the political police, to assure his safety, often spread false rumours about the time of his departure. They say it is 2 p.m.; then 11 a.m.; then 6 p.m. Finally it is put forward to 4 p.m. when he really departs. One day Kadar asked his security chief to come and see him. He told the man: 'It's enough to tell *me* the real time.'

All these anecdotes are pleasant and intelligent enough to add up to quite an attractive portrait of the rarest type on earth: a Communist leader with a sense of humour. But my point is this: the gentleman I talked to did not wish to convince me that Kadar was a great leader, an eminent Marxist–Leninist, an astute politician and a statesman of stature; he was only concerned to prove to me that Kadar was a funny chap.

My moment of truth came when I visited a charming old prima donna of the operetta. She is seventy-eight years old, still lovely, still on the stage and still the rage of the country. We were invited to lunch in her large, elegant house. She has a lovely view from her balcony – everyone has a lovely view in those parts: with Sydney, Budapest is one of the two cities where, sooner or later, you are bound to suffer from acute view-poisoning. There was a younger woman – an ex-actress called Betty – among the few guests who kept praising, adoring and admiring our hostess. The prima donna *was* charming, an excellent hostess and a wonderful woman for her age; but this incessant flattery was nerve-racking. Betty repeated at three-minute intervals that the old lady was the most beautiful, talented and famous woman in Europe, that no one had ever played any of her roles even half as well, let alone better; that the food in her house was the best in the country, her recipes were fabulous, her paprika-chicken tastier and her beer colder than anyone else's; that her *barack* – the apricot brandy which she had bought from the local grocer – was stronger, older, better than the *barack* anyone else bought from the same grocer. English actors and actresses love flattery too, of course, but the subdued tone makes the whole thing more bearable. English flatterers don't say: 'You are superb, you are divine . . .'; they say: 'In that part, Gladys, you were pretty good, you know,' to which Gladys replies modestly: 'Well, I must admit I wasn't quite so displeased with myself as I usually am.'

The prima donna was a shrewd woman and she was not taken in for a moment. She assessed herself – her numerous virtues and few defects – as objectively as any actress could. Perhaps she even felt a healthy contempt for her sycophant and was fully aware that Betty must feel a healthy contempt for her. But what could she do? She needed this flattery just as a drug-addict needs her injection. The drug-addict may hate heroin but cannot live without it.

Two or three hours of this and I caught myself red-handed, or red-faced. The attitude was contagious and I found myself talking just like Betty. 'But you are great . . . you *know* you are inimitable . . . Miss So-and-so played the goose-girl in that operetta better than you? Nonsense! No one can ever do it half so well . . . You are the queen of them all . . .'

And then I began to understand my irritation with the people of Budapest. Their silly boasting, their obsessive wit, their lack of sincerity – was it not my own faults that I was detesting in my brethren? If three hours in this prima donna's company had turned me into an old-fashioned Central European gallant, then there, but for the Grace of God, go I.

STATUES

YOU are busy telling yourself for the fiftieth time that the town is shabby and dilapidated when suddenly a worrying thought strikes you: how shabby and dilapidated are you yourself? When you tell a Hungarian teenager that you knew poets like Atilla Jozsef and Miklos Radnoti well, they look at you much as an English or American boy would if you told him that Byron and Shelley used to be chums of yours, or that you played cricket for Canterbury with Chaucer.

Walking along a street in Buda, you remember Hungary's great humorist, Frederick Karinthy. Here on the corner used to stand the café he visited every day and where, at frequent intervals, he got into debt with the head-waiter, being unable to pay his bill. Then you discover, with a start, that the street itself is now called Frederick Karinthy Street. And somewhere else you see another street named after another friend who used to be unable to pay his bill in another café. Yet another one reminds you that a third friend still owes you five pengoes, but as he, too, has now been turned into a street, you haven't much chance of seeing your money. With a largish square you once had a drunken fight at three a.m. in the City Park and that statue there – so majestic on his pedestal – used to go to bed with one of your girl-friends. It hurt very much at the time – it was certainly not the behaviour you expect from a statue.

Then you get a real shock. Old So-and-so has become a *boulevard*. Not just a street, a close, a crescent, or even a square: a *boulevard*! When former friends become streets, you are pleased and proud; when one of them becomes a *boulevard*, you fall silent and think of eternity.

JOKES

THE history of Hungary began with a joke. When we were small boys (I have mentioned this once before*) we were taught about the conquest of Hungary by the ancient Magyars. The conquest was never called by that name: it was always described as 'the Foundation of the State'. The founder himself was an individual always referred to as 'Our Father, Arpad.' Our Father Arpad with his wandering Magyar tribes arrived at the Danube in the ninth century. Present-day Hungary was then inhabited by Slavs. Our Father Arpad sent some cheap gifts to Svatorluk, the Slav ruler, and in exchange asked for a piece of earth, a bucket of water and a few blades of grass. When Our Father Arpad's seemingly modest wishes were fulfilled, he declared that Svatorluk had forfeited his country, having symbolically handed over his land, with all his rivers and pastures. The king of the Slavs replied that there must be some misunderstanding and tried to explain: Our Father Arpad, however, took the land and chased the king away.

For quite a few years I was deeply convinced that Our Father Arpad had played a dirty trick on Svatorluk. But later I realized that I was wrong. Our Father Arpad was a medieval gentleman of impeccable character and he played no dirty tricks on anyone. He was joking. He had a tremendous sense of humour and the Hungarian penchant for jokes was founded then and has flourished ever since.

Whatever happens in Hungary or the Soviet Union – or in the rest of the world, for that matter – Budapest's response is a joke. However frightening and horrible an

* *Milk and Honey*, André Deutsch.

event is, Hungary's response is a funny story. This is not due to coldness or frivolity; it is a natural, defensive response which has raised the status of the joke to that of a minor art and a political weapon. A joke in England or America or Holland is a joke, a funny story to enliven an after-dinner speaker's performance. In Hungary a joke is a sedative and a blow against tyranny.

Take any event in the period of post-war Hungary.

Compulsory adulation of the Russians started immediately after the war. Soviet culture was superior to Western; everything, from the bicycle to television, was supposed to have been invented by the Russians (usually by a man called Popov); to be born Russian was the happiest fate imaginable. The Hungarians listened to these teachings in silence and with scepticism, for they had witnessed the primitiveness, brutality and poverty of the Red Army and of some Russian officials. The story went round:

'What was the nationality of Adam and Eve?'

Answer: 'They were Russians. They were hungry, went barefoot and naked, had to steal apples when they wanted to eat, yet they insisted that they were living in Paradise.'

The terror became more and more unbearable: mock trials, the execution of innocent people and the extortion of false confessions were the order of the day. Budapest remembered Attila, the Hun – but not in any derogatory way: the Huns were cousins of the Hungarians, we were always taught to hold them in high esteem and I was genuinely surprised when I learnt that in England *Hun* was a rude nickname reserved for the warlike Germans (actually a stupid and boastful pre-World War One utterance of the Kaiser was responsible for this usage). In Hungary we were taught that when Attila died, his body was put in a threefold coffin and sunk in the Danube. Every so often a threefold coffin turned up and violent debate ensued as to whether the remains were those of the King of the Huns. It was said at the height of the Rakosi terror that another one had been discovered, but this time there was not a shadow of doubt about it: the body *was* Attila's.

'But how can you be so sure?' people asked.

'He confessed,' was the answer.

The most horrible moment in Hungary's post-war history was at dawn, 4 November 1956. Shortly before, the country had been deliriously happy, thinking that they had managed to get rid of the Russians. But in the early hours of that Sunday morning, the Russians returned, breaking their word; tanks and artillery opened fire at buildings where peaceful citizens were asleep, killing many of them. The Russian-controlled radio kept on issuing statements telling the population to remain calm because the Russians were coming as friends.

'Thank God,' was Budapest's wry comment. 'Imagine how they would behave if they were coming as enemies.'

The bulk of the jokes are less gloomy. I interviewed an old friend, Ivan Boldizsar, an editor and writer, for my television-film, and he told a current joke:

'Why don't Hungarian workers ever strike?'

'Because nobody would notice the difference.'

'And why don't Hungarian workers work?'

'That's tradition. In Hungary the ruling class never works.'

Or there is the joke on pure ideology. A gipsy musician goes to his band-leader (the *primas*) and asks him:

'I say, one hears these words so often – but I just don't get them. What the hell are Capitalism, Communism, Socialism and Reaction?'

'It's quite simple,' replies the band-leader. 'Say a guest to whom we play gives us a hundred forints. If I keep it all, that's Capitalism; if I share it out equally among us, that's Communism; if I invest the whole lot in a new violin and nobody gets a penny out of it, that's Socialism. And if anyone dares to utter one single word against this, he is a bloody reactionary.'

The year 1970 – as already mentioned – was the centenary of Lenin's birth. The radio, television, newspapers talked of almost nothing else for a year, no political speech was delivered without repeated sycophantic references to Lenin, songs were written and plays were performed in his honour until the whole country was suffering from acute Lenin-poisoning and the mere mention of the man's name produced a yawn coupled with nausea.

'What great event occurred in 1873?' asked Budapest.

'??????'

'Lenin was three years old.'

*

Thus in Hungary the joke has great social and political significance – as it had for the Jews oppressed under the Tsars. The Jews in Tsarist Russia were persecuted, kicked around, looked down upon, yet remained convinced – with reason – that they were no worse, no less valuable human beings, than their coarse uneducated and corrupt oppressors.* Their only means of saving their self-respect, indeed of surviving, was to laugh at their tormentors.

Something very similar happens in Hungary under the current tyranny; and, of course, Budapest humour has a strong sprinkling of Jewish wit in it. Under oppressive régimes jokes replace the press, public debate, parliament, and often even private discussions – and they are better than any of these. They are better because a serious debate admits two sides, two views; a serious debate offers arguments and permits rejoinders. But the joke is a flash, a thrust with a rapier – it is as one-sided and tyrannical as the tyrant's own utterances. The joke makes a fool of the tyrant, pricks holes in his pomposity, brings him down to human level. Every joke seems to weaken the tyrant, every laugh at his expense feels like a nail in his coffin. No one living in the atmosphere of a western democracy can imagine the liberating and invigorating effect these jokes have as they spread from mouth to mouth. The régime is fully aware of the current jokes. Kadar – from what I hear about him –

* These ideas have also been expressed in my book, *Humour in Memoriam*, Routledge & Deutsch. I notice that I keep quoting from my earlier books. Intimate familiarity with one's sources is a sign of true scholarship.

insists on being told the latest, not only because he wants to know what is going on but also because he enjoys a good laugh. The régime tolerates and encourages these jokes – some of the rulers, too, are numbered among the clever chaps of Budapest. The joke may well feel like a nail in the tyrant's coffin but it is also a safety-valve and thus it helps to protect the very tyranny it aims to destroy. This is true to form: smiling tolerance of jokes may look like convincing proof of liberalization; in fact it is a clever trick of a tyranny which has undoubtedly mellowed.

Budapest jokes are a blessing – yet they have a curious by-product. The city's reputation as the Jokes Capital grew and grew until it became a pose and an attitude. Now Budapest believes that whatever happens in Hungary, in Czechoslovakia, in the Middle East, or anywhere else, the world will turn to Budapest, awaiting its comment in jokes. They feel they *must* produce *the* joke. They don't believe that a breathless world waits for the President of the United States or the First Secretary of the Communist Party to speak; that it hangs on the reaction of the world press, or NATO's next move. What it waits for is what the jesters of Budapest are going to say. When you meet a Hungarian after a shocking political event, he will say: 'Have you heard the latest?' – he and his compatriots are slowly becoming the club-bores of the world. The jokes are often good; but too often again they are a rehash of old chestnuts, a bit faded and pale, like everything else that becomes smug, self-conscious and oracular.

What am I driving at? Is the Budapest joke a Good Thing or a Bad Thing? Am I for it or against it?

It is a Good Thing and I am for it. Their sense of humour is the saving grace of the people of Budapest. It is the grace that saves their dignity, occasionally their sanity. Yet, alas, it is impossible not to notice that a quarter of a century of frustration, tyranny and fear has not increased the sense of fun and ebullient jollity.

*

I should like to conclude this chapter with a joke which was the current favourite during my last visit. It is one of the thousands of Lenin jokes.

For the great centenary the cuckoo-clock makers of Moscow decided to add something to the glory of the occasion by holding a competition. The third prize was won by a clock from which, when it began to strike a cuckoo popped out and said: 'Lenin! Lenin!' The second prize was won by a clock from which a cuckoo popped out and shouted: 'Lenin has lived! Lenin lives! Lenin shall live!' The first prize went to a clock from which Lenin popped out and shouted: 'Cuckoo! Cuckoo!'

FOOD

It was the morning coffee served to us in the Royal Hotel on our first day which compelled us to move out. I had been dreaming of good Budapest coffee with the pleasure of anticipation: it used to be delicious. The horrible dishwater served in the Royal was more than a disappointment: it was an eye-opener, not without political significance.

When I speak of 'horrible dishwater' I do not simply mean that I personally did not like the coffee there; I mean that it was foul by any standards. It was sour, as if the coffee grounds had already been used several times. Subsequent investigations proved this to be the truth. Hungarian – all East European – workers are so underpaid that pilfering has become widespread. Honest people who previously would not have dreamt of stealing are driven to it now, in spite of heavy, occasionally savage, penalties. They do not even feel guilty: they are being robbed by the state, they say, so they are simply rectifying an injustice. Pilfering in restaurants and canteens is notoriously easy everywhere. Hungarian law prescribes how much coffee must be used to make a cupful. Check-ups are frequent and retribution for breaking the rules harsh. So canteen staff do not dare to use less coffee than prescribed, but some of them, anyway, mix fresh coffee with yesterday's grounds, half and half. Try making a cup of coffee for yourself following this recipe, and you will see what I am talking about and will grant that the adjectives 'horrible' and 'foul' reveal admirable restraint on my part.

So it was principally this coffee which drove us away from the Royal – one of Budapest's expensive luxury hotels.

We rented two rooms in a private flat and this may have been the first mistake which led to my subsequent expulsion. All hotel rooms are bugged – indeed, in new hotels microphones and other bugging devices are built in as the building goes up, the price being included in the builder's estimates. The private house I moved to was un-bugged and the police may have suspected a dirty trick on my part: I meant to keep my private conversations private. Not at all; I knew of the bugging and took it as part of the game that when in a hotel room I must speak of the Soviet Union, their occupying forces, and the Hungarian political police in the warmest terms, with deep affection, often with tears in my eyes. I simply wanted to drink decent coffee in the morning.

I felt outraged about that coffee and whenever you feel outraged – not simply annoyed or irritated, but morally indignant – always examine yourself. Moral indignation is the most suspect and revolting among all human reactions: the moralist, when carried away by strong and noble feelings, should always examine these feelings most critically. This time, too, the fault lay partly with me. (This does not acquit the coffee: it *was* filthy dishwater.) I had to realize that I was still a stomach-patriot.

In most things (after thirty-three years in Britain) I have become much more English than most Englishmen. In some respects the Duke of Devonshire or a colonel of the Brigade of Guards can take lessons from me on how to be English. But some things are ineradicable. I have already spoken of my poetry-patriotism: poetry means only Hungarian poetry for me. (This is not literary patriotism, only poetry-patriotism. As far as prose writing goes, Hungary is a small nation with a small literature – some of it very fine – but four or five of their poets belong among the world's giants. The world, alas, has to take my word for that – few people in it are competent to check up on this seemingly extravagant claim.) Another pocket of resistance is football-patriotism. This surprised me when I discovered it. I am not particularly interested in football and detested it as a child: I hated the huge, dirty ball swishing and whizzing towards me and was afraid of the big boys, tackling mercilessly and kicking me on the shin. The Hungarian national team came to England in the early fifties, to play a game subsequently labelled 'the match of the century'. A few days before that match, I talked to Arthur Koestler who asked me which side I supported. The very question surprised me. I told him I was a British subject now, a British patriot and – naturally enough – I was supporting the English side. He shook his head and said: 'Patriotism is one thing; football-patriotism quite another.' I did not follow. But a few days before the match I began to waver. On the great day I was driven with Vicky – the lovable and great cartoonist who died such a tragic death – to Wembley. Vicky was another Hungarian and our English colleagues in the car started teasing us about the terrible thrashing Hungary was going to get. That decided it. We made bets all round, wanting the Hungarians to win. The match started and the Hungarians scored a goal within thirty seconds. Vicky and I stood up and applauded. Never in my life had I been so near to lynching. To applaud in the press box is bad form; to stand up and applaud is worse; but to stand up and applaud the enemy side is one of the most heinous crimes imaginable. The great match was the talk of the town for quite some time and both Vicky and I were strutting around as if we had scored all six Hungarian goals in person.

The last field on which I remain an unrepentant Hungarian patriot is food. During the first few days of my visit memories and wishful thinking proved stronger than reality. Apart from the breakfast in the Royal Hotel, all my meals were pleasant emotional occasions for me. This was Hungarian food, full of the tastes of my childhood, cooked and prepared in Hungary. I noticed that the BBC chaps were somewhat reticent in their praise. They were aware of my enthusiasm and when I praised the magnificent meals we were having, they nodded and said: 'Quite.' My companion – a great expert on food – said even less. In a few days I was driven to face stark reality: the food was indifferent, it ranged between the mediocre and the lousy. We had some magnificent meals in private homes but that's a different story.

The reasons for this decline are not difficult to see. First, almost all restaurants are State-owned and there is no competition (food in the few small privately owned restaurants is much better). Secondly, we were there at the height of the tourist season, when every place was chock-full whatever muck they served. Thirdly, the material they are using is third-rate. Fourthly, more and more people are eating in cheap office and workshop canteens and fewer and fewer people bother to learn how to cook. The dominant taste of the Hungarian kitchen is paprika. All dishes had the required paprika taste and this was enough to make many foreigners – mostly Germans – think they were eating magnificent Hungarian food. In all fairness, I ought to emphasize that I interviewed dozens of German tourists and they all said: '*Ja, sehr gut, sehr gut.*'

If by any chance the food is acceptable at one or two places, the service spoils it. Service is universally awful – at least during the tourist season. I do not know what it is like in December but in August it has to be seen to be believed.

We arrived at the Busulo Juhasz (The Melancholy Shepherd) restaurant at 8.00 p.m. We had to wait for a table till 9.00 p.m. (which was our own fault, we had failed to book). Our order for three portions of fried chicken and some wine was taken at 9.30 p.m. *Two* chickens arrived at 10.10 p.m. We asked the waiter: what about the third? He said he was frightfully sorry, he did not know how he could make such a silly mistake but he would order the third now. What about the wine? Oh yes, the wine. The wine arrived at 10.40 p.m., the third portion of chicken (mine) at 11.25 p.m. This experience was worse than average but only slightly. At Gundel's – once the pride of Budapest, today a mediocre place with stiff prices – the waiter persuaded us to choose a certain dish – the speciality of the house and particularly good that night. I ordered it only to be told thirty-five minutes later that they did not have it. In the Café Belvarosi we got chipped glasses – but the girl did at least warn us to drink from the unchipped side, otherwise we would cut our lips. In the Nador at Pecs they have the Russian system which means that one poor, over-worked and over-tired girl works while three pompous managers supervise her. The result is that having waited the usual half-hour for our breakfast, we had to wait another thirty-five minutes for the bill – and got our orange-juice at the end of the whole procedure, after payment. At the best hotel at Veszprem the table cloths were disgustingly filthy, the potatoes uncooked, the fish cold – and if you did not like this you could go to another restaurant, owned by the same firm, the State. I could continue this lament indefinitely. We did have tolerable service once or twice – but this was the rare exception. Shops are no better than restaurants, indeed worse.

I had often heard, before arriving in Hungary, that waiters and shop-assistants were rude. I must say I never met with any rudeness. Exasperating inefficiency exists along with extreme, often embarrassingly feudal courtesy – still very much in fashion in Hungary – or with sighs of resignation. One gets the impression that waiters have too much to do, and with tips understandably in mind, are fighting a hopeless battle against bad organization and an inefficient – often malicious – kitchen personnel who are jealous of the waiters and do their bloody best to deprive them of tips.

Having spent a few weeks in Hungary, I was expelled from the country (for reasons to be related). This expulsion was by no means a pleasant experience but it had some agreeable facets. One of them was that after arriving in Vienna I could go to a restaurant and have a really good Hungarian meal.

GATYA NATIONALISM

BEFORE the war the Hungarian image was that of a romantic and eccentric people, perpetually listening to gipsy music, furiously dancing the *csardas* – Hungary's national dance – the whole night long and at dawn, with a final eruption of yet more boundless energy, kicking the roof off the inn.

The bandleader, the *primas*, went from table to table, playing romantic tunes close to the ladies' ears and was rewarded by the ladies' male escorts, who spat on the banknotes before sticking them to the *primas*'s forehead. The gipsies were often hired for serenades: a young man, or even on occasion an old man, courting a lady would position the band at 3.00 a.m. under her window and order them to play her favourite tune. It was touchingly romantic, except that it advertised their relationship to all and sundry, woke up the entire district and angry, elderly or jealous neighbours, wanting only to sleep, occasionally emptied the contents of a chamber-pot on to the serenader, thus diminishing the romantic effect of the performance.

Nearly everyone abroad has heard about the *puszta*, the endless, monotonous Great Plain, with its picturesque draw-wells, where beautiful, fierce, wild horses gallop about, eventually to be tamed by the *csikos*, Hungary's own cowboy or gaucho. The *csikos* and other Hungarian peasants wore the *gatya* – a word to be pronounced more or less as it would be pronounced in English – white, wide-bottomed trousers, rather like long, Victorian under-pants, an extremely comical garment. When I went abroad as a young journalist foreigners seemed to be surprised that I did not gallop up to the door on a wild horse from the *puszta*, passionately playing a gipsy violin, with my *gatya* wildly waving in the wind. This *puszta*-and-*gatya* nationalism annoyed us no end; it was a false picture, deliberately cultivated by the régime and hardly fitting in with the poverty of the thirties, with pale, unemployed workers starving in unheated, miserable rooms and all sorts of intellectuals – qualified doctors, lawyers, engineers – leaping to their deaths from the Danube bridges because they could not find a job and their future looked bleak and hopeless. But the splashes announcing their demise were muffled by the jingling and tinkling of duelling swords and the tear-jerking melodies of gipsy serenades.

One of the good things the Communists did was to abolish this *gatya* nationalism. Duelling was out, serenading became ridiculous and semi-criminal and the *puszta* was turned into agricultural settlements; even the gipsies were renamed folk-musicians.

But then in the sixties tourism began to rear its ugly head and the need for hard currency became pressing. The Hungarians looked with envious and incredulous eyes on Spain, and even more so on Yugoslavia, two formerly poor countries, made rich by tourism. The Hungarians were determined to get tourists – but how? Who would want to come to Hungary, they asked each other dejectedly in the early sixties. Who would come to a country notorious for the Rakosi terror, the Mindszenty and Rajk trials and, above all, for the Revolution of 1956, so ruthlessly and treacherously quashed by the Russians? But the régime was growing more liberal and was determined to show a more civilized front to the world. This front *was*, indeed, growing more civilized and tourism, eventually, had a further liberalizing effect. Yet, the question lingered on: *who on earth would want to come to Hungary?*

The answer was obvious but painful: Hungarians abroad, first and foremost, those 200,000 young men and women who had escaped during the Revolution and who would like to visit their parents, sisters, brothers, aunts and friends.

But was it possible to let these people in? Hungarian economists – a brilliant lot, appreciated all over the world – came up with an astonishing doctrine: the dollars brought in by these refugees would be just as hard as the dollars brought in by any White Anglo-Saxon Protestants descended from the Pilgrim Fathers. And the same applied to pounds sterling, German marks and Dutch guilders brought in by former refugees who had left the country a few years before.

To allow these people in was a bold political decision. They often arrived in large, new cars, showing off, swaggering and bringing gifts to their poor relations which they distributed in a patronizing or ostentatious manner. Many of them were vulgar; even the most modest and best mannered among them were detested and envied. When a visiting '56 refugee – now a waiter in Frankfurt – was unlucky enough to run over a child with his huge white Mercedes, the whole country was up in arms: 'they' come home, the bastards, to kill Hungarian children! Deep-seated emotions were stirred in every heart; yet nothing could disguise the fact that these traitors and renegades grew rich in the capitalist west in no time, while true patriots and loyal Communists – or people who had hesitated too long and missed their chance to get away – sweated their guts out in the Socialist Paradise, often doing two or even three jobs to make a living, and got nowhere.

Slowly, however, they *were* getting somewhere. Partly because these renegades helped the country with their foreign currency. Appetites were whetted: tourism had to be developed properly. Refugees coming to visit Dad and Mum were helpful but not enough; *real* foreigners were needed, in search of the exotic.

The inevitable followed. Those fiery philippics against feudal gimmicks were forgotten. The folk-musicians were called gipsies once again but now they were dressed in red, green and yellow sham-Hussar uniforms (never worn by them even under Horthy) to please the executives from Mainz and the vice-presidents from Cleveland. The *puszta* (which was rapidly becoming a normal agricultural and horse-breeding area) was turned back into the romantic Magyar prairie – into the Bugac and Hortobagy of the *Betyar* (the highwayman, the Hungarian Robin Hood), with the *csikos* riding his wild horse, his *gatya* flapping in the wind. In other words, *gatya* nationalism was revived with a vengeance – becoming more ridiculous, more incongruous and greedier than ever before. Hungarian food deteriorated and service became a bad joke (see chapter on Food) but the sweet smell of *paprika* overhung the country and visitors poured in by the thousand and loved it. Rakosi, Rajk, Cardinal Mindszenty, 1956, and the political police – the Avo – (which had seemingly gone into liquidation) were forgotten; the visitors drank the pleasant, sweetish Hungarian wines, sang newly-learnt Magyar songs, danced the *csardas* accompanied by gipsy music, visited the *puszta*, tried to ride the beautiful, wild horses and bought a pair of *gatya* to take home to Phoenix, Arizona and wear on appropriate occasions as casually as a pair of *gatya* can be worn in Phoenix, Arizona. Tourists flocked to Hungary, and the government felt embarrassed and ashamed: they knew that – whatever Marx and Lenin may have taught them – their most successful economic stroke was the revival of *gatya nationalism*. Hungary is not a beautiful country, no rival of Austria or Yugoslavia, and the few really beautiful parts – some hills in Transdanubia or the Matra – are hardly ever visited by tourists. The swimming in Lake Balaton is excellent, the water pleasant, soft and caressing to the skin; but the scenery around it is dull, monotonous and almost depressing, with the exception of perhaps two points, Tihany and Szigliget. The visitors come to hear the gipsies, eat goulash, see the *puszta* and other contrived tourist attractions – the whole show being as representative of Hungary as the Venetian gondolier, singing *Santa Lucia*, is of the starving Calabrian peasant or the Mafia. The tourists have poured millions of dollars into the country; and the government has blushed. They were blushing all the way to the bank.

Duelling is still forbidden but, no doubt, will return in time and chivalrous Communist knights will fight each other in public with heavy cavalry sabres three times a day, admission $2.50.

Hotels spring up in the tourist areas from one day to the next. Some are better built than others. We stayed in one, called The Lido, in Siofok on Lake Balaton. This was the hotel's first season but it was already in a state of disintegration: out of ninety-eight tiles originally covering the bathroom wall twenty were missing, or irreparably damaged, discoloured or broken; the shower was wobbly, squirting water everywhere except on the desperate hotel guest standing underneath it, hoping to get wet. Walls were cracked. The building (unless miraculously saved at enormous expense) will become a slum in no time. But it is the present that matters – the German tourists who turn the place into a German colony; who spend their revalued marks lavishly bringing well-being in their wake.

There is nothing particularly wrong with all this, and the determination to make a quick buck is, unlike the *gatya*, not a Hungarian speciality. The greed of these Leninists may be surprising; their reverence for the despised dollar may seem incongruous. But it is not unique. Some high official once said that modern tourism was like the Crusades: it brought people together. Meditating later on his words, I found them most appropriate: yes, the Crusades, I nodded. The number of people moving around was incomparably greater today than in those medieval times but the vulgarizing effect must be about the same. This time, however, it is the Crusader who is robbed, not the land through which he passes. And modern tourism has about as much to do with the spreading of true Christianity as the Crusaders had.

I do not condemn the Hungarians for their eagerness to fleece the tourist. Show me the land where the growth of the tourist industry is unaccompanied by the growth of the milking-the-tourist industry. But the whole phenomenon makes me wonder. In a world where the British imperialists have voluntarily given up their colonies while the Soviet Communists have established a new colonial empire; where the great economic success of scientific Hungarian Marxism is to revive Horthy's *gatya* nationalism at its worst; and where – at the same time – a British Conservative government has nationalized Rolls-Royce – could we not understand each other just a little better? Or is it possible that, in fact, in quite a number of ways, we understand one another only too bloody well?

SCHWEIK IN BUDAPEST

'I HOPE they give me a visa,' I said to one of the Hungarian Ambassadors on the Continent, while I was actually waiting for it. 'If they let me in in 1964 they can't possibly have any reason for keeping me out today. Besides, they know that while I shall criticize certain things, I love the country and shall not be really hostile.'

The Ambassador, who was listening to me carefully, replied with a broad grin: 'If you promise to be really hostile, you can be sure of being let in.'

He was right, of course. What he meant was that the last thing the Hungarian government wanted was yet another testimony that Hungary was a nice, civilized, almost Western country, very different from the other satellites, where life was as pleasant and freedom as prevalent (or almost) as in Sweden. What the Hungarian government would have preferred was written testimony (to be shown to the Russians) that they provided a nasty, orthodox Communist tyranny, were maniacal devotees of Marxism–Leninism–Brezhnevism and that life in Hungary was hardly distinguishable from life in Uzbekistan.

'What happened to Schweik?' is a question often asked about Czechoslovakia – Schweik, the 'good soldier', innocent and willing, who could never be convicted of a crime but unfailingly managed to sabotage Austria's war effort, and who is the only great literary figure the Czechs have given the world. The answer is obvious: he has surreptitiously crossed the Czechoslovak frontier and moved into Hungary. He is vociferous in protesting his loyalty and devotion to Brezhnevism–Kosyginism while he is dancing the *csardas*, Hungary's national dance: two steps to the left, two to the right. Except that when Brezhnev isn't looking he slyly changes the dance a little: one step to the left and three to the right. The rhythm remains the same.

I do not wish to give the impression that Hungary was or is the land of light-hearted gaiety and joyful liberty. A great deal has been written about the terror-ridden days of Rakosi and there is no need to go over this subject in detail, once again. It will suffice to say that I had about thirty friends in London during the war – Communists, Socialists or a-political lovers of their homeland – who returned to Hungary after the war. Twenty-six of them were imprisoned on trumped-up charges, beaten up, tortured and kept in jail between five to seven years. Another went mad under the pressure of protracted questioning under torture. The greatest shock for him was that his loyalty to the Cause had been doubted. He protested his loyalty loudly; a shade too loudly, in fact. He was beaten to death by the truncheons of AVO thugs while he was shouting: 'Long live Stalin! Long live the Soviet Union!' He was a sweet and gentle person, an able poet. The twenty-eighth was given a high position – well, nearly all thirty were at first given high positions, but this man fared particularly well because his brother was the deputy chief of the AVO (the secret police). When his brother fell from grace during the Rajk upheaval, both men were arrested. Eventually they were both pushed *alive* into a bath of acid and perished, literally without a trace. The twenty-ninth was hanged after a mock trial for industrial espionage of which he was completely innocent. The innocence of all twenty-nine people was eventually established, they – or their widows – received grudging apologies and small sums in compensation for the torture, humiliation, beatings, lost years and lost teeth, kicked out by the jackboots of the AVO. Only my thirtieth friend had a lucky escape. He was among the very first to go home. He boarded a plane in Croydon, full of hope, enthusiasm and optimism for a new, justly governed

Socialist Hungary. His plane crashed soon after take-off and he died. Lucky devil.

But people like to remark that those times are over. Those were the times when 'Socialist Legality' was admittedly broken; those were the days of 'the Cult of Personality'. One is struck by the elasticity of Communist phraseology. When anyone deviated from the true creed in the minutest, most insignificant and often even non-political detail, he was called a Japanese spy, an imperialist hyena. Yet when those admitted horrors, the hanging of hundreds of completely innocent people, beatings, tortures, acid baths are recalled, the most English of understatements is brought into use: all this was just 'the Cult of Personality'. Not even the Cult of a Sadistic, Paranoid, Monstrous Personality. Simply, and modestly, the Cult of Personality.

But, of course, all the horror did not end with Stalin's death. The Hungarian Revolution and the Kadar terror followed. The Kadar terror never reached the depths of earlier times. There were executions and there were concentration camps but it was never as bad as the Stalin terror; it was as pleasant and gentle as, say, Horthy's White Terror after 1919 – one of the darkest periods of oppression, yet differences in degree are extremely important in such matters. Kadar still has to explain to posterity how he – a Minister in Imre Nagy's revolutionary government – betrayed his chief and became the Russians' stooge and why he connived at the execution of Imre Nagy on Hungarian territory, about two years later. No light matters, and the explanation – if and when it comes – will not be too easy. Nevertheless, this same Kadar has proved himself to be a good and humane man, a miracle of survival, an astute politician, a Hungarian patriot, a man of decent instincts and of liberal tendencies, a man with a sense of humour and anyone who denies that Hungary's lot has improved under him beyond all expectation is either a fool or an undaunted warrior of the Cold War. Even deadly enemies of the Communists dread the eventuality of Kadar's death or fall. But Hungary remains a

Russian-occupied country. Thousands of Russian tanks and hundreds of planes are the custodians of Socialist law and order – and the AVO (now under a new name) still has other duties than directing traffic and looking after the welfare of tourists. The Russian forces are always referred to – if mentioned at all – as 'temporarily stationed in our country'. They arrived in 1945. The rule of the Habsburgs was also temporary in Hungary. It lasted four hundred years.

In any case, by now, Schweik has arrived in Budapest where he has more or less taken over the reins of government. Schweik is no novice in Hungary. During the war – from 1941 to 1944 – Hungary had a Prime Minister, Miklos Kallay, who was perhaps the champion fence-sitter of all time. While he was reassuring the Nazis of his unwavering loyalty, sending troops to the Russian front and making anti-Semitic noises, he protected Jews as much as he could and made an agreement with the British and the Americans not to fire at their planes while they, in turn, promised not to bomb Hungarian territory. When a few American bombs *were* dropped, Kallay protested (through devious neutral channels) to the Americans, who duly apologized. All this in the middle of the war, between belligerent powers. If Kallay was the best pupil of Schweik, Kadar is the best pupil of Kallay – with one great similarity and one even greater difference. The similarity is that both Kallay and Kadar were true Hungarian patriots. The difference is their attitude *vis-à-vis* their masters. Kallay was no Nazi. He hated the Germans and everything they stood for. Kadar is a convinced and honest Communist, a believer in the creed, and the Russians have every reason to trust him.

How does this modern Schweikism–Kallayism work today? Simply and effectively. It has two basic rules:

1. Pay the loudest lip-service to orthodoxy and go on your way experimenting. Before introducing a semi-capitalist measure, explain that this is a new blow being struck for true Leninism.

2. In foreign politics follow the Russian line fully and

faithfully; thus you will gain great scope for manoeuvring in internal politics.

*

Just a few examples. In 1968 the Hungarians introduced a system called the New Economic Mechanism. The gist of it is decentralization and autonomy of planning. Each enterprise will have to be profitable and self-supporting. One of the founding fathers of the system explained to me that this was no step backwards towards Capitalism but, on the contrary, a further courageous advance towards Socialism. Not even a reform of Socialism; but true, orthodox Socialism. After all, nothing has been given back to private enterprise – Central Planning has just been replaced by Regional Planning. Profitability? Socialism – he went on – was never against profits. No economy could survive on permanent losses. Profit was one thing, *private* profit another. It is true that now managers and workers *share* in these profits. I pointed out to him that the share of managers and executives was huge (up to fifty per cent) while the share of workers was small (about fifteen per cent) and asked: would this system not increase the existing gap between rich and poor?

'Oh no,' said the economist. 'Don't you see that if the manager of an enterprise works at a loss, he will have his income actually cut while the worker can only gain? So the managers carry a much larger responsibility and this responsibility warrants higher rewards.'

This, of course, answered my original question positively: yes, the new system *will* increase the existing gap between rich and poor. The justification for this increase – the reference to the greater responsibility of managers – was an old-fashioned capitalist argument. Yet the economist maintained that the New Economic Mechanism had nothing to do with Capitalism: it was realization of true Socialism. Criticism – inside an enterprise – was encouraged, new ideas welcomed. Firms worked better and produced more; the possibility of Socialist gain was a great incentive. (Socialist gain used to be called *profit*, I thought: not exactly an invention of Karl Marx.) But – he went on – overall planning remained and profit was not everything. General Motors or Ford may have individual workshops which work at a loss for the benefit of the whole firm or for prestige reasons, but the firm *as a whole* must be profitable; in the same way, the economy of Hungary *as a whole* must be profitable.

I was a little surprised to hear General Motors and Ford quoted, instead of Engels or Lenin, but all I said was: 'Surely, all this resembles the Yugoslav system very closely. Do you agree that but for the Yugoslav example, you would not have your new system at all?'

'I admit that we have learnt a great deal from the Yugoslavs. Yet the Yugoslavs have gone too far and decentralized madly. They have become too *anti-dogmatic*.'

I looked at him and asked if it was possible to become too anti-dogmatic.

'Of course it is,' he said. 'In many cases *anti-dogma* itself can become a new dogma.'

They have an answer to everything. And often a clever one. And their industry is flourishing and Hungary – unlike Britain – is doing better and better every year.

*

Or take just one further practical example of this neo-Schweikism. This story comes from 'usually' – indeed unusually – 'well-informed sources'. During the Dubcek period Brezhnev and Dubcek had a twelve-hour quarrel because Dubcek had told the Russians that he wanted to reintroduce a modicum of private enterprise. Small firms – up to five or ten employees – should be allowed to do certain, specific jobs better suited to small enterprises. Brezhnev was outraged; he ranted and raved. He banged on the table. He said that was letting Capitalism in through the back door. It was a betrayal of Socialist principles, etc, etc. No one says that Czechoslovakia was occupied *because* of this plan; but this suggestion certainly figured on Dubcek's crime-list. All the Warsaw Pact satellites had to send troops to participate in the occupation. The Hungarians did so too – they too punished Dubcek for his plan to revive private enterprise. The Hungarians never mentioned that they had, in fact, introduced this Dubcek system years before and up to 300,000 Hungarians were engaged, at the moment of the occupation of Czechoslovakia, in private enterprise. The tremendous difference was that the Hungarians had never asked permission from Brezhnev and did it on the quiet; and if they had anything to say about it, they called it a further bold step towards Socialism.

*

Perhaps it is the gentle Kallay whom the Communist Kadar imitates; perhaps it is the Czech Schweik who became naturalized in Hungary; or perhaps we are simply witnessing the old art of attempting to have your cake and eat it. If anyone is accused of practising this art, he protests indignantly instead of being proud of his skill. It is one of the great aims of my life to have my cake and eat it. Alas, I rarely have it; and when I eat it, it often gives me indigestion. So I admire my Hungarian ex-fellow-patriots for practising the art of having it both ways with such consummate skill. They are the most reliable of all satellites (second only to East Germany) yet they follow Yugoslavia and openly adopt capitalistic practices; they deviate from the Sacred Book while protesting their utmost devotion to it; their great ideal, they vow, is the Soviet Union, yet they do their utmost to remain a Western land; they took part in the occupation of Czechoslovakia for *trying* to introduce private enterprise which they themselves had introduced some years before.

And yet . . . is one justified in thinking that these clever Hungarians can fool those stupid Russians and lead them by the nose? Is it really likely – or indeed possible – that several thousand Russian observers, staying permanently in the country, fail to see what every casual observer notices during a brief visit? The suspicion slowly dawns on one that it is not the Hungarians who are using the Russians but the Russians who are using the Hungarians. As long as they do not breach *fundamental* laws (and Dubcek and Imre Nagy tried to breach the most sacred of those basic principles) the Hungarians are *encouraged* to make certain experiments. The Russians want to see how certain ideas work out in practice and what reaction they provoke in the West. In this dirty business of politics – as so often happens East of Calais – it is, once again, a little difficult to see clearly who is fooling whom.

(And when I come to think of the British elections of 1970 – smug, patronizing self-confident Harold Wilson, and 'poor Ted' who was thought to have been beaten even before he started – it is not always too easy to see it West of Calais either.)

YOUTH – OR THE MEMORY OF A REVOLUTION

'THIS vast army of fanatics who spread the Communist creed with discipline, oppression and torture are all unbelievers to the last man.' These words were spoken by a Polish intellectual, Czeslaw Milos, who had chosen freedom at the height of the Stalin terror in the early fifties. I cannot find the quote but the argument made a great impression on me at the time. His point was that there were then something like a hundred basic tenets of the creed and anyone who rejected – or even doubted – any one of them was guilty of deviation and liable to arrest, dire punishment and, possibly, execution. But there was *not one single man* in the Soviet Union or Central and Eastern Europe who believed it all (*all* means everything that *Pravda* wrote and the local, satellite *Pravdas* copied); not even Stalin. To doubt, for example, that Zinoviev and Co. were really traitors and agents of foreign intelligence services, probably meant death to the doubter in those days. But Stalin knew perfectly well that Zinoviev, as well as hundreds of thousands of others, died on trumped-up charges; he trumped them up.

Today the mood has changed. The reign of terror, in its Stalinist form, has disappeared; people in Hungary can voice certain criticisms (see next chapter) and the horror of the knock on the door at dawn does not haunt the ordinary citizen. To doubt one scintilla of truth in the creed is no longer a capital crime – although doubting certain basic principles still is. Russia has become even more unpopular, because nationalism has become stronger all over Eastern

Europe. Romanians, Hungarians, East Germans, Poles all hate the Russians; even the Czechs have turned against them after 1968. It is only the Bulgarians whom they can trust.

What happened? The basic answer is simple and twofold.

First, a great many people's interests became inextricably involved with the régime, which has now been in power for over a quarter of a century. There are civil servants, army officers, policemen, politicians, journalists and a horde of other people whose livelihood is bound up with Communist power. They still do not believe that, say, 1956 was a Counter-Revolution, or that the Hungarian army when invading Czechoslovakia was doing a service to a fraternal state where Socialism was threatened by a few wicked enemies of the people; but they want to *live*. A change would not simply mean difficulties with their jobs but, in many cases, instant dismissal and – for some – imprisonment. The 1956 Revolution made short shrift of AVO men by stringing them up on lamp-posts; people – not unnaturally – wish to avoid even vaguely similar inconveniences. Sheer economic interest ties thousands of people to a régime they detest. The passing of time has compromised further thousands who – although out of sympathy with many aspects of the system – have had to pay lip-service, have had to act as loyal party-members and are by now regarded as such and are hopelessly compromised. The more detested the régime becomes the more this army will help it: they have more to fear from a change from the *status quo*. Yet while the Russians are becoming increasingly unpopular, the régime is not – not in Hungary. Many things have improved and go on improving. Hungarian Communism has acquired that human face – or human mask – Dubcek was talking about. (There is a small minority of irreconcilables, of course. To them nothing seems good, all Party members are knaves and fools, nothing has improved since Rakosi's days and anyone who says a word in praise of Kadar is either an idiot or a traitor to Hungary.)

But the attitude of youth is much more interesting and

important. Young people in Hungary do not seem to be rebellious. They are not against Socialism and it would be difficult to find one single individual among them who wishes to return to Capitalism. The rat-race, the real-estate speculators, the stock-exchange society, the greed and materialism of the West repel them. But the well-being that Capitalism creates attracts and excites them. Western youth is fed-up with consumer goods, fast racing cars and package tours. Hungarian youth wants more consumer goods, more and faster cars – and dreams of package tours. Western youth hates the Good Time Society: Hungarian youth longs for a good time.

But the young people's acceptance of Socialism does not mean uncritical acceptance of Brezhnevism or even Kadarism. They are not sheep and are as intelligent and as nonconformist as their fellows abroad.

But their morale is low. One lament I heard from them was the loss of ideals. 'We have nothing to fight *against* and little to fight *for*,' an intelligent law-student complained to me. 'Yes, we accept Socialism – but what are we to do about it? Socialism is here and that's that. The older generation boasts about their struggles and achievements; we simply *exist*. We accept the prevailing ideology and observe that it does not really prevail in practice. A man who gets a university education still enjoys class privileges – even if they are not called class privileges any more. Physical work still stinks but nobody says so. Our socialism is a lie and we hate lies. But to fight for "truth" and "honesty" is too vague, too general. It's not an ideology. It's a naïve dream.'

I talked to many others. They accept the Socialist superstructure and there is no negative agitation, no counter-revolutionary feeling among Hungarian youth; there is, however, a wave of indifference. They are not anarchists; they are simply bored. There are small activist groups of course. Some call themselves Maoists, but in Hungary Maoism simply means anti-Sovietism, so becomes, curiously enough, the equivalent of Hungarian nationalism.

There is a minority who are deeply interested in politics. They stand to the left of the régime, regard it as a bourgeois, bureaucratic system and want real Socialism. They are Leninists, not Brezhnevists; they are no Trotskyists but admire Rosa Luxemburg. They watch developments with despair: a new class of lawyers, engineers, physicians, economists and other graduates run the country, a new bourgeoisie has taken the place of the old. They approve the Brandt–Brezhnev pact because they want peace and *rapprochement* with the West; but many of them recall the Ribbentrop–Molotov Pact, in other words, they suspect just another cynical, tactical move. What they say is that in two and a half decades of Communism a new Establishment has taken over and the game they play is based on new rules; but they, the young, reject all rules and all games, they long for ideals, they long for a little honesty and truth. Kadar is clever enough not to dismiss these young idealists as being beneath notice. He approves of their '*responsible* impatience', meaning that impatience is befitting to youth, but no active expression of this impatience will be tolerated.

The whole past for teenagers is a Communist past. They remember no other régime. Young Germans after the war asked their parents: '*How could you do it?*' When young Hungarians ask that same puzzled and troubled question they are referring to the Stalinist era. They listen to the explanation of their elders about errors, misjudgements, the crimes of Stalin, the Cult of Personality and fail to understand the unintelligible, fail to accept the unacceptable. Just as the post-war young Germans rejected their parents' apologies for SS atrocities and extermination camps; just as the youth of Israel failed to grasp the docility of *their* parents in the concentration camps.

Another intriguing question is: what does the 1956 Revolution mean for the youth of today? Even leading Communist politicians – not the young, but the old – who would still speak of 'counter-revolution' (a completely discredited, and highly offensive term) admit that 1956 was a failure. It was their failure, first of all, for not foreseeing the dangers; it was a failure, they say, of the Revolution itself which did not achieve its purpose and eventually set the clock back; it was a failure of communication; a regrettable or – according to the most rabid of them – a shameful event. Clever propagandists of the régime dismiss the wild talk about shame and would never use the expression 'counter-revolution'. It is unnecessarily provocative. But, they maintain, the present régime has achieved everything that – and more than – the Revolution hoped for. Today Hungary has consumer goods, foreign travel, a certain amount of freedom of expression, tourism, even the good old jokes – so what else can one wish for?

If you point out that one could wish for real freedom, true democracy, a political opposition, self-determination for Hungary and the end of Russian occupation, they smile and call you naïve and unrealistic. Their thesis is that Hungary has achieved everything one can realistically hope for and the Revolution, far from helping, only delayed the achievement of all this. The truth is, of course, that without Khrushchev's de-Stalinization there would have been no Revolution; but without the Revolution a lot of these further improvements would never have been attained.

I had expected that the Thirteen Days That Shook the World would have been a great, traumatic experience for the country – but this is not so. For Western Europe and for Hungarian refugees abroad these events mean more, the experience is more alive, than for most people in Hungary. Even these people who whole-heartedly supported the Revolution are far from over-enthusiastic about its glory. For them too it was an event which ended in failure and disaster. They achieved nothing; they suffered afterwards; they were left in the lurch by the West. I still believe the Hungarian Revolution was one of the significant, inspiring and hopeful events of this century, but most people in Hungary – even those who otherwise share my basic views – would disagree with me. They are perplexed and embarrassed; they may have inspired the world but they achieved nothing for themselves; the world applauded but failed to help; the world had tears in its eyes but *they* had to suffer.

The attitude of adolescents and university students is the most surprising of all. The truth is that the Revolution means little to them because they were too young to participate. Youths of eighteen or twenty were toddlers of four or five in 1956. The Revolution lasted for less than a fortnight and made little impression on them. They have heard a lot of official propaganda and balderdash which most of them are intelligent enough to reject without, however, being able to arrive at the truth. In any case, the Revolution of 1956 is a historical event for them, like the World Wars, or the Revolution of 1948 or the story of Our Father Arpad.

The great, traumatic year for this student generation is not 1956 but 1968. This date may mean little to the average English or American reader. Well, what happened in 1968? A lot. The French student revolt happened and the occupation of Czechoslovakia happened. Both events caused tremendous excitement and made their ineradicable impact. They also spelt out their moral only too clearly. France 1968 taught them that revolutionary youth can change the fate of the world; Czechoslovakia 1968 taught them that it cannot.

THE TRUE PATRIOT

'WE are Socialists but we hate the Russians,' a boy of eighteen told me. 'We are not Titoists, but we want the Russians out of here. There is very little we can do about it.' Then, after a short pause, he added: 'But that little we do.'

'What do you do?' I asked.

'We do what we can to show the Russians our displeasure.'

I did not understand. If there had been the slightest manifestation of hostility or any demonstration against the Russians, it could not have remained secret.

'We are a small group of patriots. Not really organized or anything. There's one thing we can do. We go round at night and pee into the petrol-tanks of cars with Russian number plates.'

'You are joking.'

'I am not. Many Russians know about it. They park their cars in well-lit squares under the lamps. Or try to get locks for their petrol tanks. But many others know nothing about it. And then, in the dark, we pee into their tanks.'

I recalled the petrol on sale in Hungary in 1964 and thought that a little pee would have improved its quality. But those days were over.

'It's not much,' the young man added, 'but we do it.'

'I am glad the spirit of the Revolution is still alive,' I answered somewhat wryly.

'Ours is not an ideal way,' the boy went on modestly. 'Not a noble way. We are a small group only. And girls, however enthusiastic, are prevented from giving free flow to their patriotism.'

Free flow, I thought, was the *mot juste.*

HOW LIBERAL?

When I visited the Foreign Ministry in Budapest, I was always offered Coca Cola. How liberal can you get? I asked myself in astonishment. How far can a Communist state go in bowing to the achievements of Western civilization?

The Hungary of the seventies is a different, pleasanter, place from the Hungary of the fifties. It is easy to find evidence of liberalization; it is equally easy to find evidence that all this liberalization is a fake, no more than an eyewash to blind the West and Western tourists.

But improvements remain improvements. If you do not have to live in fear of the police; if you can open your mouth and criticize certain matters; if you can get a passport and travel abroad; if there are two candidates to vote for instead of only one – then life becomes more bearable. To deny all this would be unfair; yet nagging doubts remain.

Many of the new freedoms are quite obviously sham ones. The régime proclaims that everyone is entitled to a passport today and can obtain it without difficulty, which is true, but they forget to add that a passport does not entitle you to go abroad. You cannot go without it; but a passport is not enough. You need an exit visa from the police and this is refused to critics of the régime, recalcitrant elements and nonconformists. So you can get the document, but you have to deserve your permission to go abroad. Or perhaps it would be more correct to say you must not do anything to jeopardize your chances.

People – good, reliable, loyal people, that is – are allowed to go abroad once in two years and to take $100 worth of foreign currency with them. The customs are very liberal in not making strict inquiries when travellers – having spent four weeks in the West – return with $500 worth of goods. Everybody has an aunt abroad and Hungarian aunts seem to be the most generous race on earth.

'There is no censorship in Hungary,' quite a few journalists told me. This is not true: films, plays and books *are* censored, and writers may be sentenced to shorter or longer periods of silence. Any literary work may be mutilated or changed, and plays are sometimes banned. Literature is freer than in the worst days of Socialist Realism but the degree of outspokenness, of criticism, of rebellion is officially regulated. The degree of deviation is controlled; revolutionary writing is licensed by the authorities. It is true that there is no pre-publication censorship of newspapers, but this means nothing. The threat of retribution and subsequent punishment is enough. Besides, party hacks in editors' (or deputy editors') chairs receive strict instructions about the 'line' and see to it that it is followed. *Internal* censorship is the most effective.

I saw one real and surprising sign of liberalization. In the Kerepesi Cemetery of Budapest – Hungary's national cemetery – young freedom fighters of 1956, most of them teenagers, are buried and their tomb-stones carry the inscription: '*Died a hero's death*'. A few yards away about two hundred secret-police victims of the Revolution are buried in more splendid and impressive graves and their tombstones speak of the 'nation's eternal gratitude'. It is possible that the government attempted a generous gesture of reconciliation – but that's exactly the point. Stalin or Rakosi never attempted any reconciliation at all. It is surprising to see that the freedom fighters (who are occasionally still called counter-revolutionary bandits) are buried in graves of honour and described publicly as having died like heroes.

Anti-Semitism has also faded – more or less – and is not officially encouraged. Hungary today is no Poland or Czechoslovakia. It was the Russians who, after the liberation, put three Jews and one non-Jew (Rajk) in power and subsequently instructed the Jews to hang the non-Jew, eventually blaming the three Jews (a) for being Jews and (b) for killing Rajk. It would be foolish to state that anti-Semitism is dead in Hungary. Hundreds of thousands of Jews were murdered by the Nazis and their Hungarian henchmen during the war. Anti-Semitism is an archetypal, atavistic, hatred *of the self* and modern anti-Semitism needs no Jews. This is a surprising discovery, for which the credit goes to the Poles. There are hardly any Jews left in Poland but anti-Semitism flourishes. Perhaps the Poles were encouraged by the example of the medieval church: they had witch-hunts for centuries although there were no witches. Hungary today follows Russia's pro-Arab policies and quite a few old fascists and ex-Nazis believe that 'anti-Zionism' is making anti-Semitism respectable once again. Zionism is becoming a bogey. The secret police is after 'pro-Zionists' and many politicians accuse their Jewish colleagues of being 'pro-Zionists'. A young man visited me and 'interviewed' me for over an hour about my views in connection with Israel. It was only by chance that I learnt that he was not a journalist but a police-agent, sent to catch me out. As I have written two books on the subject, they could have 'caught me out' with less trouble by reading them.

In the 1971 parliamentary election (this is only a plan at the time of writing) Hungarians will not have the customary single list but will be able to choose between two candidates. This does not mean the appearance of an opposition. All candidates must accept the aims of the Patriotic People's Front, in other words, the Communist Party. Secondly, out of Hungary's 349 electoral districts only a fraction will have the benefit of a choice. So the liberal character of this reform is more apparent than real. And yet . . . it goes further than anything known in the Soviet sphere; it is a step in the right direction; it is a curb on little local Caesars: it will no longer suffice for them to please the party potentates, they will also have to court their constituents.

20 August is a national holiday in Hungary. It used to be St Stephen's Day. St Stephen was a descendant of Our Father Arpad, and brought Christianity to Hungary. For a long time after 1945 St Stephen was anathema, nevertheless 20 August remained a national holiday. It became Constitution Day, to celebrate the new Communist Constitution of Hungary. The year of my visit, 1970, was significant for two reasons: it was, as already mentioned, the centenary of Lenin's birth; and it was also the first time that St Stephen could be again mentioned publicly as Stephen the First. He was deprived of his sainthood but became mentionable; and 20 August was celebrated as the Day of the Constitution *and* Stephen the First's Day. I listened, in Parliament Square, to the main official speech of the day, delivered by one of the ministers: he mentioned Lenin seventeen times, Stephen the First once and the Constitution not at all. But if this was only a glimpse of the Saint – and under a pseudonym at that – he had slipped back into public life.

One could mention many other examples. I feel the question: *is liberalization in Hungary real?* ought to be answered with a *yes*. It is enough to sense the atmosphere in the country to realize that people breathe quite freely and are either satisfied with their lot or, at least, resigned to it. Hungary is proceeding, however slowly, in the right direction; she is walking, and walking slowly, rather than driving, but she is nearer to and not farther from the goal. Western observers are often astonished when Hungarians boast that there are no more arbitrary arrests. Is that such a boon? People who have lived through Stalin's terror are grateful for small mercies, and know that it is indeed a boon.

The snag with this liberalization is not that it is not real; but that it is strictly controlled from above. It goes exactly so far as the authorities permit, and no further. Opposition is tolerated; rebellion is licensed. The game has its rules and as long as you know and follow them you are safe. Criticism? Oh yes. You may criticize the lack of veal on the market; the clumsy distribution of new potatoes; the litter in the parks and the infrequency of trams. Funny men on the stage are allowed a few cheeky remarks against government policy and the audience is allowed to applaud. Should the jester go too far he will be kicked in the pants. One television programme is permitted to interview ministers of the second rank on administrative questions (bad housing or insufficient hospital equipment) in a tough, semi-Western manner. This criticism gives the impression of freedom and acts as a safety valve at the same time. Anyone who can blow his top will calm down afterwards. So far so good. But no one in his senses would dare to utter a word against the Soviet Union; or hint that the Soviet occupation forces might go home; or propose the foundation of an opposition party; or say that Kadar should resign; let alone suggest that Hungary should leave the Warsaw Pact and join NATO. All this would be against the rules and would amount to sheer lunacy.

Little wonder that people are divided on this issue of liberalization. The more gullible – and that means the overwhelming majority – are pleased; they are taken in. Things are moving from less freedom to more; from one candidate to two; from no criticism to some; from rampant police terror to the political police trying to keep discreetly in the background. These are real benefits, not to be scoffed at. Yet the less naïve and more pessimistic hold different views. They say that controlled freedom of speech is no freedom of speech at all. If you are not allowed to say what you like, only what you are allowed, where is the freedom? As a disillusioned ex-Communist told me:

'Certainly it is better to be allowed to say *something* rather than nothing. Certainly it is better to be allowed to travel abroad once in two years – provided you are a good, obedient fellow – rather than not to travel at all however assiduously you may lick the boots of party-leaders. Certainly, two candidates are twice as many as one, even if both are Communists and are carefully vetted before being permitted to stand. But there are no constitutional safeguards. Our freedom – such as it is – is not a right, merely a loan or a whim. I should not call our country free; but I am delighted to admit that it is the gayest hut in the great Russian concentration camp.'

HOW TO BE AN UNDESIRABLE ALIEN

My one and only day-dream has always been to become a famous international spy. I owe the fulfilment of this dream to the authorities of the land of my birth. Admittedly I had no life-and-death struggle with Mr Aranyi – an official of the Press Department – on the parapet of a balcony on the eighteenth floor of the Foreign Ministry; I was not chased through the sewage-system of Budapest; I did not swim the Danube underwater; and never – this is a special regret – did I have to wear a false beard; but I *was* called a Master-Mind and that compensates for a great deal. For a few hours I felt like the legitimate successor of James Bond.

The story of my expulsion from Hungary is one of the minor historical events of this century. Still, it is worthwhile recalling it briefly because it has a moral and throws a truer light on modern Hungary and her liberalization, than the gipsy bands dressed in red velvet mock-Hussar uniforms, the wild horses of the *puszta* or the wild tourists of Lake Balaton.

When Michael Houldey, the producer of my BBC programme, and I arrived in Budapest we were told by the Hungarian television people that we would be given a permanent escort – somewhat euphemistically called a Production Manager. This did not surprise us: we knew that Hungary was, after all, a Russian-occupied satellite and not a Scandinavian democracy. But there are police spies and police spies. Some of them are delightful. Ours belonged to another category. He lacked the charm, wit and warmth one associates with top police spies and, to make matters worse, he was unreliable and inefficient. He was supposed to make appointments for us but the appointments were not made; he was supposed to make arrangements for the 20 August celebrations, to get passes for us to Parliament Square and for our cameraman to film the parade from the roof of a near-by Ministry. The passes he procured were no good. The cameraman never reached the top of that Ministry and we were chased from pillar to post by angry soldiers and policemen.

It so happened that a few days later I lunched with Mr Aranyi, a newly appointed member of the Foreign Ministry's Press Department. I asked him to give us another police spy. We were ready to accept one; we were keen on having a police spy; we insisted on a police spy. But we wanted one with slightly more engaging manners or, at least, a more efficient one. Mr Aranyi was much concerned. He told me that the relationship between the BBC and Hungarian Television had not been so intimate and loving as might be desired. It had improved lately but should I come forward with a request for a new police spy, this might cause bad blood. He suggested a compromise: we were about to go to the country, to Siklos (my birthplace), Lake Balaton, the *puszta* and other tourist places, and we needed no police spy on that journey. I agreed: we could manage without a police spy. But – Mr Aranyi continued – on our return, for the last week, when we would do political interviews and more serious stuff, we should have to put up with him. Fair enough, said I, a true British compromise. I drank another glass of official Communist Coca-Cola, shook hands, and, a day or sc later, left for the country without our police spy.

He did not like this. As he had arranged to bring his girl-friend with him, at our expense, he liked it even less. (I was somewhat puzzled by that girl-friend. She looked like a typical Charles Addams woman who had escaped from the pages of the *New Yorker* and had been granted political asylum in Hungary. Later I became convinced that she was actually spying on our police spy, and for him to go about without *his* official spy would have been as much a breach of the regulations as for us to go about without ours.) Our Man, therefore, ran to his bosses, the political police, and told them that he had been left behind. The police were outraged – they demand respect for their informers. When it turned out that we had acted on the instructions of the Foreign Ministry, the matter became even worse, turning into an inter-departmental squabble between the police and the Foreign Ministry. It had to be made clear who was master. And when it comes to the crunch, the masters of the country are the policemen and *their* masters are the Russians.

So it was decided that I must be expelled. But they could not expel me on the grounds that I had left my officially appointed police spy behind: that would never do for the new liberal image. A frame-up had to be arranged. In such cases the police decide what form the crime is to take. They are a good and efficient force, they can frame you for anything. The commonest charges are: currency offences (it is child's play to plant a few dollars on you to prove some illegal transaction which in fact you never carried out); sex crimes (raping girls of under six years old is very popular); and spying. Spying is the most respectable of these, and I am eternally grateful to the police bosses for finding me worthy of this type of framing.

While we were driving from Kecskemet (a small town south-east of Budapest) to the *puszta* a car followed us. We first noticed it at Bugac, in the *puszta*, standing under some trees with no one in it. Having finished our work at Bugac, we were on our way back to Kecskemet when Michael Houldey noticed some hay-making in progress. He thought it a romantic sight and stopped to film it. He reversed BBC car number one about a hundred and fifty yards down the main road. Passing traffic had to stop or slow down, and hooted at him furiously: in other words he called a great deal of attention to himself, which is an old trick of really cunning spies, so that they can say later: 'Is a spy likely to behave like that?' BBC car number two, with the sound-engineer in it, and car number three, in which I was travelling with a friend, stayed about a hundred and fifty yards away and took no part in the proceedings. The cameraman, his assistant and the producer got out of their car, set up a tripod and started filming. A few minutes later two policemen pounced on them and told them that they were filming at a place where photography was forbidden. They had driven up in the car we had seen under the trees at Bugac, and proceeded to escort us to Kecskemet police station where we were kept for three hours. Our film was confiscated but we were treated with courtesy.

At this point I must explain that at some places in Hungary (and in other Communist countries) there are signs by the roadside which say PHOTOGRAPHY FORBIDDEN. They also show a camera crossed out with a red line. I used to think that their purpose was to draw the attention of enemy agents to good spying places – 'You should look around *here*', they were saying: 'we have hidden a vital secret near by' – but I was wrong. The real purpose of these signs is to help the police frame people. We were told that we had deliberately ignored one of these signs, and it was pointed out to us as large as life, fixed to a lamp-post. How was it that seven of us, three of us at the wheels of cars and all of us well aware that we must watch out for such signs, had missed it? The truth is that the sign was put up *after* the crew had started filming. I heard later that this is a popular trick, and an old one: it was *vieux jeu* in Russia even in the twenties, with the variation that in the Soviet Union people were shot in the nape of the neck after such a frame-up while I was only expelled from the country. Later, people were to explain to me that the difference is purely theoretical. A country where the police are not engaged in pursuing wrongdoers but in framing innocent people, I was told, is not civilized, and its police are no better than a gang of criminals. I could not agree. I was able to discern a real difference between being shot dead and being firmly asked to clear out. On this occasion, I admit, I realized that liberalization in Hungary was much more real than apparent.

The day after our encounter with the Kecskemet police we were summoned to Mr Aranyi, who told me that I was *not* expelled – oh, not at all – but merely requested to leave the country within twenty-four hours. I told him that the essence of a request was that it was open to the requestee to comply with it or not. Did I have a choice? Mr Aranyi told me most emphatically – and with somewhat sinister undertones – that this was a different type of request and I had no choice. Then, said I, I would prefer to call it expulsion.

Mr Aranyi told me that I was indicted on three main charges. (1) We had left our police spy behind. I replied that we had done so on his, Mr Aranyi's, advice – to which he failed to reply. (2) We had been filming in places which had not been mentioned in our original plans. I told him that this must be a reference to our filming the graves of Freedom Fighters in Kerepesi Cemetery. My attention had been drawn to the existence of these graves by the Assistant Editor of *Nepszabadsag* (Hungary's local *Pravda*) who had encouraged us to film them, and special permission to do so had been obtained by Mr Aranyi himself. To this Mr Aranyi also failed to reply. (3) We had been filming at a forbidden site. I told him that we had missed the sign (at that time I still believed that we had committed a genuine mistake) and that in any case, the mistake had not been mine. I had taken no part in the filming and was reading in my car about a hundred and fifty yards away, innocent as a lamb. Mr Aranyi implied in his answer that guilt had nothing to do with Hungarian justice: I was the Master-Mind so I would have to go, although the BBC team – who *had* committed the 'crime' – was implored to stay. I felt infinitely proud, because I had never been called a Master-Mind before. The BBC crew, on the other hand, must have felt slightly offended, or even jealous, that *I* had been granted this distinction, and to show their displeasure they left the country with me.

*

What is the moral of this ludicrous incident? It offered a better insight to the working of Hungarian democracy than anything else I encountered. Scratch the surface, however lightly, and underneath the gaiety, the gipsy music and the *bonhomie* you find the police-state. The whole affair was most clumsily conducted: the police were unable even to pretend that I had committed the 'crime' of taking pictures of hay-makers; Michael Houldey, the leader of our group, was in fact the dangerous Master-Mind behind this crime, reluctant though I am to grant it, and the police themselves admitted that I had been some way from the scene. But something always sticks. Ferenc Molnar, the playwright, once said: 'Never touch shit, even with gloves on. It is never the shit that gets glovey; it is always the glove that gets shitty.'

The police improved on their story later, but it took them quite some time. Weeks after my departure they started spreading the news that I had been working 'for another organization' and had actually been filming a Russian military airfield. The first part of this allegation is true. I was, in fact, working for quite a few 'other organizations': the publishers André Deutsch Limited in London, Gambit Inc. in Boston, Econ Verlag in Düsseldorf and – with a bit of luck – Penguin Books and a few others. But anyone who believes that a set of spies would go to work as openly as we did (or rather, as the BBC team did, because I *didn't*), would believe anything; and anyone who thinks that when a group of people is caught filming a Russian military airfield, the Russians are satisfied with expelling one innocent man and do not even question any of the people involved, or mention the charge to them . . . well, Mr Greville Wynn and a few others could tell a different story. The confiscated film has been seen by the Hungarian police and by people from Hungarian Television. Budapest being the most gossipy town in the world, I know that the television people's comment was: 'This haystack looks like a haystack and nothing else.' But since I have now accused the Hungarian political police of framing me – in other words, of behaving like a bunch of criminals – perhaps in their own defence they might care to show this film to a group of neutral television people who could tell the rest of us whether they can detect any sign of a military airfield – or just two peasants making hay. I solemnly promise herewith a reward of £1,000 to anyone who can point out one single Russian aeroplane, however small or smudgy, on that film. Indeed, on second thoughts I increase the offer to £1,000 per plane.

Quite a few Western friends, having read of my experience in newspapers or heard me recounting it on television, have told me that they have changed their minds about going to Hungary and will spend their next holiday in Switzerland instead. Others, still anxious to go, have asked me whether they should. Well, nine hundred and ninety-nine persons out of a thousand will fare all right and will, indeed, be charmed by their visit. Few people, after all, have made a film of the Hungarian Revolution and written a book about it, as I did. Anyone with a similar record should go to Cap d'Ail instead. Minor motoring offences such as running over a dog or a sheep are punished with uncivilized severity, so do not run over a dog or a sheep while in Hungary. If they have something against you, they will frame you. A 1956 refugee against whom they are alleged to hold a grievance got drunk and, having exhausted his supply of Hungarian currency, gave a five-dollar bill to the gipsies who had entertained him. He was given four years. In fairness I must admit that I have no first-hand knowledge of this incident, and that although I trusted my informant he may have got it wrong; but unfortunately my own experience has made me only too ready to believe this type of story. And such an incident might spoil one's holiday.

Many people – newspapermen, radio-interviewers and friends – have asked me: what does it feel like to be banished from the country of one's birth for ever? It is not pleasant to be thrown out of any country, and if it happens to be your native land – which you still love and whose son you still feel – it becomes no pleasanter. Nevertheless, I am used to the feeling of leaving Hungary for ever. I have done it many times. In 1938 I left for good, only to return in 1948. During the Rakosi terror I felt sure that I could never go back, but I did. Having returned during the 1956 Revolution and having written a book about it, I was convinced that my break with the country was final, but I was invited to return. After my most flattering *Encounter* article they were deeply offended, but they let me in again. Now I have been expelled for good, of course. But how long is eternity? In a country where Rajk was the chief terrorist and Minister of the Interior for a while and was subsequently hanged; where Rakosi once was God and was then refused permission to return from Russia and died in exile; in a land where Kadar was a member of the government, was then sent to prison, and later became ruler of the land; in a country where people are not left alone even after their death (Rajk was reburied and Stalin - in a neighbouring country - was expelled from his mausoleum): in countries like that decisions do not remain valid for ever.

According to a popular story Kadar and his high-ups visit a town and are petitioned to allocate some money for a new school and a new prison. He allows five thousand forints for the school and one million for a modern prison. One of his colleagues asks him: why this huge discrepancy and this bias in the prison's favour? Kadar replies: 'Because, gentlemen, we are unlikely ever to go back to school.'

Well, one day, when not only the Russian-controlled police but even the Hungarian Foreign Ministry will have a say in the country's affairs, I may return; I may even be invited to go back. But so long as the present gentlemen run the country, or until they return to school or somewhere else - although I still love the country, its language, its poetry, my friends - I am not tormented by nostalgia.

*

My expulsion was not an altogether agreeable experience. Having been told to leave, some extremely unpleasant hours followed. We moved around a bit and were followed and watched from every possible angle. The street we lived in was suddenly swarming with plain-clothes men, who stood on the pavement in languid attitudes, wearing coloured shirts and ostentatiously advertising their lack of interest in me. Another horde of policemen was watching the BBC team in their hotel. When Michael Houldey and I wanted to have a private word we had to walk around the park to be sure of avoiding big ears and small microphones. When the moment of our departure arrived, only six hours after the final interview, dozens of burning eyes were fixed upon us from all directions. On our way to the frontier we did not dare to discuss anything in our cars, for fear that they were bugged.

During that journey I thought with great sympathy and with a deeper understanding than ever before, of those millions who were staying behind. If a few hours of discomfort and, after all, not too grave danger, had provoked such anxiety in me, who am I to judge those who have to spend their whole lives in an atmosphere of stark terror alternating with liberal intimidation?

By the time I reached the frontier, I was not my splendid best. I expected a four-hour search and a lot of indignities. But the customs examination was a mere formality. The customs officer (a policeman) – the last Hungarian to talk to me on Hungarian territory before I cleared out, as ordered – asked me one single question:

'Any souvenirs?'